BECOMING NIGERIAN
IN IJO SOCIETY

■ A volume in the series
Adolescents in a Changing World

EDITED BY BEATRICE B. WHITING AND
JOHN W. M. WHITING

Project advisors:

Irven DeVore
Carol Gilligan
George W. Goethals
Jerome Kagan
Robert A. LeVine

Becoming Nigerian in Ijo Society

Marida Hollos
and Philip E. Leis

RUTGERS UNIVERSITY PRESS

New Brunswick and London

Library of Congress Cataloging-in-Publication Data

Hollos, Marida. 1940–
    Becoming Nigerian in Ijo society / Marida Hollos and Philip E. Leis.
        p.   cm.—(Adolescents in a changing world)
    Bibliography: p.
    Includes index.
    ISBN 0-8135-1360-X
    1. Ijo (African people)—Youth. 2. Ijo (African people)—
Children. 3. Ijo (African people)—Social conditions. 4. Nigeria—
Social conditions—1960– I. Leis, Philip E. II. Title.
III. Series.
DT515.45.I35H65 1989
305.2'3'089963—dc19   88-10111
                                                                            CIP

British Cataloging-in-Publication information available

■ Contents

■ Maps

■ Tables

Foreword

to Adolescents in a Changing World series
BEATRICE B. WHITING
JOHN W. M. WHITING

Few periods of the human life cycle have generated as much interest, or as much concern, as adolescence. The psychological, behavioral, and physical changes that occur at puberty are dramatic and have been the focus of much research by psychologists, educators, and sociologists. The study of adolescence has recently become a priority research topic among many private and government granting agencies, largely as a response to the increase in adjustment problems among American adolescents: alcohol and drug abuse, teenage suicide, juvenile delinquency, and teenage pregnancy. The study of adolescence is important not only because there is an urgent need to understand the socially destructive aspects of this life stage, but also because knowledge of this life stage can contribute greatly to a general understanding of the social, psychological, and physical aspects of human development in our own and other cultures.

Only recently have anthropologists turned their attention to the study of adolescence. Other than Margaret Mead's classic work *Coming of Age in Samoa*, few anthropologists have entered the field with the primary intention of conducting research on the adolescent experience in another society. While many ethnographies contain data on initiation rites, age grades, marriage practices, and premarital sexual behavior, all of which are important to the study of adolescence, the reporting of these topics has often been anecdotal in nature. For this reason we have organized and edited this series of volumes describing adolescence in seven different societies. These works are the product of years of fieldwork, data analysis, and writing by the staff and fellows of the Harvard Adolescence Project. These ethnographies will contribute to our knowledge of human development in other societies and perhaps stimulate similar research in other cultures on this fascinating stage of life.

Our interest in the cross-cultural study of adolescence is a natural outgrowth of our work on child development. Over the years we have had the opportunity to study the social behavior of children in a variety of cultures. Either individually or together, we have made observations on American Indian children, the Kwoma of New Guinea, the Yoruba of Nigeria, the Kikuyu of Kenya, and preschool children in the United States. We have also directed several cross-cultural projects on child socialization, including the Six Cultures study and the socialization part of Florence and Clyde Kluckhohn's study of values in the American Southwest. Most recently, as directors of the Child Development Research Unit of the University of Nairobi, we have had the opportunity to explore the patterns of family life among nine different cultural groups in Kenya.

Our involvement in these studies has provided us with a rich, cross-cultural data base on child development. We have learned that although there are many dramatic differences in the behavior of children across cultures, the common features are also striking. Some of these commonalities are particularly relevant to the study of adolescence. For example, in none of the cultures we have studied were boys and girls adequately prepared for the sudden surge of sex hormones that announce the onset of puberty. We have discovered that, in many respects, the socialization of children is counterproductive preparation for this event. Presumably as a consequence of the incest taboo, free and frank talk about sex is inhibited between parents and children. In none of the societies we have studied, nor in any other that we know of, do adults copulate in public. As a result, the sex act, from the child's perspective, is shrouded in secrecy and mystery.

Although adolescence requires many changes in the life-styles of girls and boys, the cultural scripts for social and economic behavior are more clearly formulated and more easily transmitted than those for sexual behavior. Since in late childhood same-sex companions predominate, learning appropriate heterosexual behavior and finding an appropriate mate are important tasks of adolescents. The hormonal changes that take place also require significant adjustment in self-image and emotions. Our studies focus on the changes in friendship formation, peer group relations, parent-child interactions, school achievement, self-image, and cognitive development.

In 1978, working with Robert Levine at the Laboratory of Human Development at the Harvard Graduate School of Education, we sponsored a postdoctoral fellow, Carol Worthman, to initiate a study of Kikuyu adolescence. A biological anthropologist interested in human growth, Carol Worthman conducted her research in the community of Ngeca, Kenya, a site where we had previously done fieldwork on Kikuyu children. While Worthman's study concentrated primarily upon the biological parameters of adolescent growth, it also focused upon the relationship between physical development and cognitive/behavioral changes. The success of this research proved to us the feasibility of conducting a multifactorial study of adolescence, thus laying the foundation for a larger cross-cultural investigation. In addition, our previous successes with the cross-cultural study of children convinced us that a similar design could be utilized for the study of adolescence.

In order to ensure the multidisciplinary nature of the project, we persuaded a group of our colleagues at Harvard to join us in planning the project. Clinical and personality psychology were represented by Carol Gilligan and George Goethals, child development by Jerome Kagan, biological anthropology by Peter Ellison and Irven DeVore, and psychological anthropology by Robert LeVine and the two of us. Irven DeVore agreed to accept the role of senior investigator.

We all agreed that the Harvard Adolescence Project should consist of field studies carried out in different regions of the world in cultures representing varying degrees of complexity. We also agreed that our sampling universe in each field site should consist of some bounded microcommunity, such as a band, a hamlet, or a neighborhood. We had used such a unit in our cross-cultural studies of child rearing, calling it a PSU (primary sampling unit). Briefly defined, a PSU is a small group of households (thirty to forty) which sets itself off from the larger society in such a way that it has some sort of group identification, shares frequent face-to-face interaction among its members, and possesses temporal and/or spatial stability. The PSU has the advantage of being the most appropriate social unit for using standard ethnographic research techniques, such as participant observation and informant interviewing.

Knowing that most ethnographic studies require a prolonged "settling-in" period during which the researcher learns the native language and becomes acquainted with the members of the community, we decided to select experienced field-workers who had already done extensive research in some other culture and who would be willing to return to that society to carry out a study of adolescence.

To implement the above plans, we applied for and received a postdoctoral training grant from the National Institute of Mental Health (grant number MH14066-06,07,08) that would support ten fellows for two years each. Additional support for data analysis was provided by the William T. Grant Foundation. The fellows chosen were Douglas D. and Wanni Wibulswasdi Anderson, Victoria K. Burbank, Richard G. Condon, Douglas A. and Susan Schaefer Davis, Marida C. Hollos, Philip E. Leis, Mitchell S. Ratner, and Carol Worthman. The field sites listed from east to west included: the Inuit (Copper Eskimo) of Holman located on Victoria Island in the Central Canadian Arctic; the Australian aborigines of Mangrove located in Arnhemland, Northern Australia; the Thai Muslim of Nipa Island located on the southwestern coast of Thailand; the Kikuyu of Ngeca located in the Central Province of Kenya, twenty miles north of Nairobi; the Ijo of Ebiama and Amakiri located in the central part of the Niger Delta in southern Nigeria; the Romanians of Baisoara located in the foothills of the inner Carpathian mountains; and the Moroccan Muslim of Zawiya located in North Central Morocco.

During the initial training period, a series of seminars were held in which the project's staff members and postdoctoral fellows gave presentations on topics relating to adolescent development. These seminar presentations proved helpful not only in identifying important issues in the field of adolescent development, but in assisting the project directors and fellows in developing research methods with cross-cultural applications. In addition, the information and insights provided by the research fellows on their particular field sites helped immensely in developing a research strategy that could be applied reasonably in all the research settings.

It was clear from the beginning of our discussions that no single definition of adolescence would serve all purposes. Since we were approaching adolescence from a multidisciplinary perspective, both the physiological and sociocultural definitions of adolescence were necessary to incorporate into the research methodology. Our basic assumption was that while the physiological changes that occur at adolescence are universal to all human populations, the social and cultural reactions to these physical maturational changes are not. Thus, while one culture may celebrate puberty publicly, subjecting individuals to a series of initiation rites and expecting a consequent change in the behavior of initiates, in other societies the physiological markers are a private matter.

Physiological definitions of adolescence, such as the interval between the beginning of the growth spurt and the attainment of full skeletal maturity or the interval between adrenarche and the attainment of full fecundity, could ideally be objectively measured through hormone assays in all the field sites. Theoretically, such physiological measures would provide the most valid comparison of adolescent maturation across cultures. Unfortunately, the logistical problems associated with such data collection as well as the social constraints encountered in most of the field sites prevented this type of data from being collected. (Only in Ngeca was the field-worker able to make such hormone assays.) As a result, we decided to concentrate upon the growth spurt for our physiological measure. Thus, the children at each field site were measured twice during the fieldwork period— once near the beginning and a second time near the end of the study period. From these measurements of height and weight the field-workers were able to calculate a growth rate for each child and from this determine his or her status with respect to physical maturation.

These measures of physical maturation were essential to obtain since we hoped to examine the effect the maturation process had upon such things as friendship formation, cognitive development, peer group relations, self-image, gender identity, and so forth. For example, does the young girl who has menstruated for the first time have a different self-image than the girl who is two to three years past menarche? Does the young boy who has just entered the growth spurt have a different gender identity than a boy who had attained full skeletal maturity? By combining our measures of physical maturation (as an independent variable) with other types of social and psychological data (as dependent variables) we hoped to address these questions for all the societies under investigation.

It was much more difficult, however, to operationalize a sociocultural definition of adolescence. Since we assumed that societies utilized different strategies for identifying and managing adolescence, it was not feasible to develop precise definitions that had any degree of cross-cultural comparability. In the end, we decided upon a broad definition: the transitional period between the end of childhood and the attainment of adult social status. This broad definition made it essential for our field-workers to examine local definitions of adolescence, which we assumed would vary among the seven cultures in our study. Thus, where one culture might rely upon physical maturation to mark the individual's transition into adolescence, another culture might rely solely upon chronological age as the criterion for entry into this stage. It was also theoretically possible that a society might not even recognize or name a transitional period between childhood and adulthood. As a result, the challenge to our field-workers was to remain as sensitive as possible to indigenous "folk theories" of human maturation.

To solve the practical problem of choosing a sample of subjects to be studied at each field site, we decided to select a single physiological marker that was transculturally recognized. The mean age of menarche was chosen for this purpose. For many of our field sites, an estimate of the mean age of menarche was available from previously published demographic and/or growth studies. For those field sites lacking such published estimates, the field-workers would have to collect data from postmenarcheal girls and women, which could then be averaged to produce an estimate of the mean age of menarche. This estimate could then be used as the anchor point for the selection of a study population that would include a group of preadolescents as well as a group of adolescents. Previous research on adolescent growth indicates that a ten-year interval centered on the mean age of menarche will include both the beginning of physiological adolescence for most of the early-maturing females and the end of physiological adolescence for most late-maturing females. Thus, for middle-class American girls for whom the mean age of menarche is thirteen, the catchment period would run from eight to eighteen years of age. Although there is no equivalent marker of physical maturation for males, we took advantage of the fact that males mature about a year later than females, and added a year to the interval used for females.

Ideally, we believed the sample size should range from eighty to ninety individuals. All of these individuals would be subjected to our physical measures of height and weight, while smaller subsamples would be subjected to clinical interviews, cognitive testing, behavioral observations, and a number of other structured and unstructured interviews designed to examine the social and psychological aspects of adolescence. Sample and subsample sizes would, of course, vary from one field site to the next, depending upon such things as community size and accessibility of informants. (The actual problems encountered in sample selection and informant interviewing were unique to each setting and are discussed in each of the volumes in this series.)

At the end of the training period, the staff and fellows produced a detailed field guide for the cross-cultural study of adolescence. This field guide represented the consensus of the research group concerning types of data to be collected and the manner of their collection. The document was developed in order to ensure a maximum degree of comparability among the field sites included in the study. The manual also suggested specific hypotheses to be tested and the methods for doing so. In line with the multidisciplinary focus of the project, we decided to draw upon the theories and hypotheses of a number of disciplines. The field manual included detailed discussions of research methodology (site selection, sampling procedures, genealogical and demographic data collection, psychological testing procedures, and methods for making physical measurements) as well as discussions on the substantive topics to be covered (parent-child relations, peer group formation, friendship, games and play activities, sexual activity, cognitive development, schooling, religious activities, pair-bonding, rites of passage, work, daily activities, and deviance).

With the training sessions over and the field guide complete, the researchers departed for their respective field sites, where the average stay was from nine to twelve months. The project directors and researchers maintained as much contact with one another as was possible, given the isolation of some of the field sites. In some cases, letters took several months to go halfway around the world. Nevertheless, all of us felt it important for the researchers to stay in contact with one another in order to share problems encountered and modifications made in the research design.

By February of 1983, all of the researchers reconvened at Harvard to begin the task of comparing and analyzing the extensive data that had been collected. Again, a series of seminars were held in which information was exchanged among all the project's participants. This phase of the research proved to be most exciting and stimulating as we saw the ultimate goals of the research begin to fall in place. Our research fellows returned with interesting observations and innovative ideas which were freely shared.

In the process of analyzing this extensive cross-cultural data base, all of us agreed that the first order of business should be the writing of a series of ethnographies providing detailed descriptions of the adolescent experience in each of the cultures. These would provide the necessary framework upon which later theoretical and comparative papers could be built.

Given the rapid rate of social change occurring throughout the world in general and in the field sites of the Harvard Adolescence

Project in particular, we have decided to call this series Adolescents in a Changing World. With the publication of these ethnographically rich volumes by the fellows of the Harvard Adolescence Project, we hope that our cross-cultural and multidisciplinary examination of adolescence will contribute a much needed perspective to this fascinating stage of human development.

■ Acknowledgments

We both share an indebtedness to a number of organizations and individuals whom we should like to mention. Then, in keeping with the separate communities that we studied, we make individual statements acknowledging the help we received, without, of course, reducing our responsibility for any errors that remain.

A cross-cultural, interdisciplinary project, such as the one of which this study is a part, encompasses a large number of individuals who participated in different ways and to different degrees. All were important, even if we should miss repeating their names here. The seminars for the Harvard Adolescent Project, both before and after the fieldwork period, received their direction and dynamic flavor from the leadership of Beatrice and John Whiting. Irven DeVore gave his name, comradeship, and good sense to the project. We are indebted to the core members of the seminar: Wanni and Douglas Anderson, Victoria Burbank, Richard Condon, Susan and Douglas Davis, Mitchell Ratner, and Carol Worthman, who were all remarkable in their ability both to share and receive ideas and opinions. We also appreciate the thoughtful efforts of Peter Ellison, Carol Gilligan, George Goethals, Jerome Kagan, and Robert LeVine, who occasionally attended the seminars and did their best to help us chart a true course in the complicated terrain of adolescent studies. Pamela Stern and Linda Kilner also joined in the seminar and contributed to the discussions. While we were at Harvard and in the field, Nancy Black, staff assistant in the Department of Anthropology, was unwavering in her attempts to unclog the bureaucratic turmoil.

All of this would not have happened without fellowship support from the National Institute of Mental Health (MH14088) and supplementary aid from the William T. Grant Foundation and the Wenner Gren Foundation. We are most appreciative of their support.

I am grateful to the officials and elders of the town of Amakiri who granted me permission to stay in the town and to study their lives and the lives of their children. Similarly, I am thankful to the principals, headmasters, and teachers of the various schools in Amakiri who allowed me to study the schools and to test and measure the students. Above all, I have a deep gratitude to the people of Amakiri who accepted me into their homes and into their lives and with their good humor and tolerance helped me through many blunders.

Although all the people who aided me in the period of fieldwork cannot be mentioned by name, I wish to express my thanks to them here, for without their help my project could not have succeeded. I wish to acknowledge special indebtedness to Chief J. O. Ariye, his brother Christmas Ariye, and their families; to members of the Omoni family; to the members of the Ekiyor family; and to the many members of the Oki family. Special thanks are also due to my assistants Laskin Oki, Friday Omoni, and Lydia Menembraye.

Apart from the people of Amakiri, my work was aided by a number of individuals to whom I am grateful: Prof. E. J. Alagoa, who officially sponsored my research in Nigeria; Profs. Kay Williamson and Robin Horton, who shared their knowledge and ideas about the Ijo with me; at the University of Benin, Prof. Michael Onwuejeogwu, Dr. Ayodele Ogundipe, who graciously received me, and Robert Meyers, who offered his hospitality. In Lagos, the family of Chief E. O. Ashamu was helpful from the beginning to the end of my stay in the country, as was Gabor Kalman and members of Medicor, Ltd. I also thank Ewi Otote, and Elke and Werner Hoffman for their sustenance and company. I am indebted to Curtis Hardyck and my niece Coco Halverson for their interest and help in my work and their willingness to share in the anthropological experience. Josiah Atemie spent many hours prior to my departure for Nigeria patiently tutoring me in the Ijo language. No words can sufficiently express my appreciation for this.

Above all, I am most grateful to the Hon. Chief Justice J. A. P.

Oki for his kindness, understanding, help, support, and encouragement during and after the field research.

M.H.

Returning to Ebiama was a homecoming for me, and I found old friends and a new generation of Ijo who were as accepting of my presence as during my earlier fieldwork there. To name each of them would go far beyond the available space, but I especially want to mention the following: the Amayanabo, Amos Yabefa Buti, Chief Rufus Akigha, Chief D. I. Igbe, F. K. Epuke, J. E. Bazighe, and Godwill Sagbeghe for involving me in their knowledge of the past and their expectations for the future of the community. Mieke Alafa, Dickson Ikeinka, Emeline Akigha, and Eretei Bazighe were unstinting friends. I am also grateful to Daveson Gede, Yawo Dickson, and Israel Kigibie for their friendship and research assistance, as well as to those whom we most depended on for our data, the youth, schoolteachers, and parents residing in Ebiama. Doikumo Ikeinka followed in the steps of his father, Governor Ikeinka, in becoming a member of my household. During my visits to Amakiri I was most appreciative of the assistance given by Chief J. O. Ariye, Laskin Oki, Friday Omoni, Lydia Menembraye, and R. T. Opukiri.

My work with the Ijo was greatly assisted by others in Nigeria to whom I am deeply indebted: Prof. E. J. Alagoa, who, as acting vice-chancellor at the University of Port Harcourt, extended numerous courtesies during the time of my research, as did Prof. Robin Horton, Prof. Kay Williamson, Prof. S. J. S. Cookey, H.R.H. W. S. Joshua Igbugburu X, and Richard Freeman. I am appreciative to Dr. Josiah Atemie for introducing me to Mr. and Mrs. Maxwell Iyama, who were most helpful during my visits to Port Harcourt and who enabled me to be graciously received in the town of Ogu. Allen and Comfort Awakessien also helped me in numerous ways. Samson and Leslie Ashamu had been students of mine at Brown University, and they more than reversed our roles in the help they and Samson's father, Chief E. O. Ashamu, gave me.

I am grateful to Prof. Sidney Goldstein for his suggestions for gathering demographic data; my study would have been more complete if I had been able to follow all of his advice.

Most of all, I am indebted to Lee Ann Kossin, who fully collaborated on all aspects of the field research. Her sensitivity to behavioral nuances was an important contribution to my understanding of Ijo social relationships.

P.E.L.

We conclude, in a sense, where we began. Both Beatrice and John Whiting read an earlier draft of this manuscript and gave us excellent advice, as did Simon Ottenberg, who was also able to give us a Nigerian view based on his own intensive knowledge of the Afikpo Igbo. We thank them for their patience and for their generous advice. We also thank Michael Rock for the drawings.

BECOMING NIGERIAN
IN IJO SOCIETY

■ Introduction

Anthropology has been in a self-reflexive mood for sometime, and it is cogent, therefore, to ask, why study adolescence? Turning the anthropological perspective on our own society, as we so often do, it is not unusual to observe—along with our consummate interest in computers and technology in general, our fickle passion for politics in passing, and our identification with screen and sports heroes in particular—that adolescence is a peculiar period of life. How peculiar is not quite clear. Just as the Samoans may have a more stressful transition from pre- to postpuberty than Margaret Mead proposed, American adolescents may not all be engaging in the anxiety of unresolved Oedipal complexes, suicidal tendencies, and lust for sex and drugs, as the lyrics of our rock-and-roll singers would have us believe. Without enveloping adolescence in more mystery than it already possesses, the questions pertaining to this transitional life period were persuasive enough to lead a group of researchers to investigate them around the world.

NIGERIA

This study is about young people growing into adulthood in Nigeria a country that itself has undergone rapid change. These two processes—the transition to adulthood, referring to the transformation of individuals, and the transition of society, referring to the

transformation or evolution of institutions and systems of meaning—
would seem to be intimately, and obviously, related. Institutions, after
all, cannot continue to exist without socialization, nor can human
individuals survive without a social context. Yet, as Tallman recently
observed, "As a practical matter . . . most [studies of] socialization
[are] not concerned with social change but with individual change.
. . . Until recently, most theories of socialization sought to explain
how people learned to fit into a particular group or social system. In
short, they were theories of conformity" (Tallman, Marotz-Baden, and
Pindas 1983, 9). From this perspective, institutions and systems of
meaning are seen as setting the stages in each society through which
individual members pass. For the most part, socialization studies
did not examine the ways those being socialized effected social and
cultural change, nor did they treat a fundamental dilemma con-
fronting all societies in a rapidly changing world: how socialization
proceeds for an unknown future that is *expected* to be different from
the present.

We look at the experiences of two groups of young people—how
their lives are affected by the choices they perceive available to them
in their Nigerian communities, and how they respond to these opportunities as they grow toward adulthood. These individual experiences
will be viewed in the context of a society that is rapidly changing in
some respects but not others.

Since independence in 1960, Nigeria has experienced an increasingly accelerating process of social and economic change as the
country moves from a colonial, agriculturally based dependency to
an independent, industrializing nation. A civil war slowed this process during the 1960s, but with income from oil the government had
ample means to incorporate the most distant and isolated villages into
the national polity. Communication networks were expanded widely
with the building of roads, and radio and television stations. Of even
more far-reaching significance may be said to be an economizing of
the mind, whereby the ideology of expectations is inexorably shaped
by participating in a global economy.

One of the major instruments of development and change is
perceived to be education. In Nigeria, as in other African countries,
"political leaders accepted the axiom that education is the basic component in nation-building and thus the foundation from which the
economic progress of Africa would spring. The reasoning was patent:
in a modernizing society where personal achievement tends to super-

sede and replace ascribed status and primordial relations, only education could open the door to political participation, social opportunities and economic advancement" (Turner 1971, 6).

Beginning in 1952 when increasing political power came into the hands of Nigerians, politicians in southern Nigeria began to call for free, universal, and compulsory education. S. O. Awokoya, then minister of education of the Western Region, declared that "education development is imperative, and urgent. It must be treated as a national emergency, second only to war. It must move with the momentum of revolution" (quoted in Turner 1971, 9). The next year, the Eastern Region minister of education presented his government's educational policy, emphasizing universal primary education. The result was a rapid growth of the school system. From 1954 to 1955 in the Western Region, school enrollment almost doubled from 457,000 to 811,000 (or from 35 percent to 61 percent of the five-to-fourteen age-group). Two years later, the Eastern Region abolished all primary school fees and primary school enrollment rose between 1956 and 1957 from 775,000 to 1.209 million, or from 48 percent to 73 percent of the five-to-fourteen age-group (Abernethy 1965, 319).

The emphasis on education continued after independence, but stress was now laid on postprimary education: the development of the secondary school system and of institutes of higher education. These were among the major goals defined by the Ashby Commission on Post-School Certificate and Higher Education of 1960, which was appointed to study the problem of educated manpower. The results of these ambitious programs were an increase in literacy among members of the younger generation, the provision of manpower for newly created positions, and a growth of political involvement. Undoubtedly, the most far reaching of the consequences was the creation of a new set of expectations among the youth coming to age under the new system. These new expectations, however, were rarely met, due to the slowing rate of economic growth and a lack of job opportunities. What O'Connell wrote for Africa in general pertained directly to Nigeria in the 1960s: "Given the sluggish rate of growth in lower job opportunities in the modern sector of most African territories, it is probable that any nation which succeeds in expanding its primary school enrollments beyond 50 percent will be faced with growing unemployment among school leavers" (1965:188).

The oil boom alleviated to some extent this unevenness in growth between educational achievement and job opportunities during the

1970s. Since then, due to the decline in the price of oil, the pace of development projects has slowed, and unemployment is once again on the rise. The commitment, however, to universal primary education and to an ever-widening secondary school network has remained the same. Young people are completing their school certificates only to find that no jobs are available for them. Their heightened expectations cannot be satisfied by engaging in rural occupations. Many of them are crowding into towns, and the observation made two decades earlier that "not enough employment opportunities exist for them and . . . they are straining housing and water supply facilities, burdening ill-paid relatives and turning to delinquency" (O'Connell 1965, 88) continues to be pertinent. The military government that seized control in early 1984 designed a new economic program aimed at mitigating the problems created by the post–oil boom stagnation. Among its major tenets was self-sufficiency, to be arrived at by introducing school fees on both the primary and the secondary school levels and by promoting a return to the land and farming occupations. To what extent these programs will shape the vision of opportunity held by the youth remains to be seen. It is doubtful that the younger generation would return to an earlier way of life, even if they were able to do so.

THE CASE STUDY

The experiences of an individual or a group obviously cannot speak for a nation. It would be an error to believe they do so for almost any large society. Nigeria, with a population estimated at 90 million and with approximately 220 different languages spoken, presents a particularly complex picture. Even when we narrow our examination to one ethnic group, the Ijo, we find a population of over a million people and a wide range of linguistic and cultural variation. The Ijo are the fourth largest linguistic grouping in Nigeria. The Ijo's occupation of the Niger Delta represents a variety of ecological adaptations and of internal adjustments to contact with Europeans and mainland peoples. They, like all other Nigerians, have been strongly affected by national independence that came in 1960 and by economic developments afforded from oil resources. We emphasize, then, that when we speak of "becoming Nigerian" we are not describing the experience of all Nigerians, or even all Ijo.

Our study is primarily a description of two Ijo communities, Ebi-

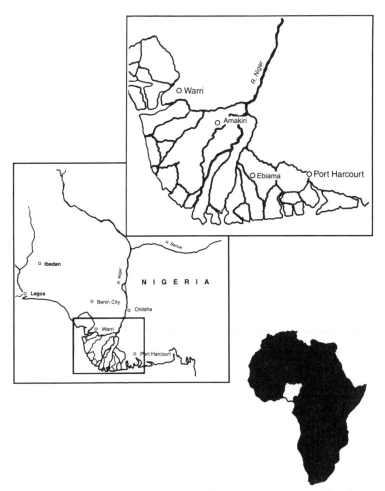

Map I.1 Nigeria. The approximate locations of Ebiama and Amakiri in the Niger Delta

ama and Amakiri; their approximate locations are given in map I.1. Both of the communities previously had been studied in 1958–1959 (N. Leis 1964; P. Leis 1972). In the restudy, M. Hollos and P. Leis are responsible for the description and analysis of data for Amakiri and Ebiama, respectively. The names of the towns and of individuals are pseudonyms.

We intend that the two towns be seen as variations on the same cultural theme. They share many cultural features, and, according to one legend, Ebiama may even have been founded by migrants from Amakiri. Ebiama is the smaller of the two communities. Located in the central part of the delta, it is accessible only by motor transport. Within the last two decades the construction of a road through the northern part of the delta has brought Ebiama to within a few hours' journey from Port Harcourt, but it remains relatively isolated compared to the larger community in our study, Amakiri. Amakiri has had extensive contact with non-Ijo peoples because of its location on the northwestern fringe of the delta. Acculturative influences, partially instigated by intermarriage with mainland neighbors and by a large weekly market, have been intensified by the construction of a road linking Amakiri to the large urban centers of southern Nigeria.

Roadways and faster types of water transports are obvious ways in which the two communities have been drawn into ever-expanding linkages with external political and economic systems. Whereas their societies could once be characterized as egalitarian and, relatively, self-sufficient, they are now beginning to be marked by social differentiation, political hierarchy, and an incipient dependency, involving daily wage laboring and insufficient food production. Their system of beliefs appears to be in a state of transition too, as Christian forms of religious practice take a dominant place in each community without wholly replacing rituals associated with local deities.

What is not so obvious in these social and cultural changes is how they are affecting the youth, who are the means for both inculcating the changes and initiating the synthesis between Ijo history and present-day Nigeria. Schooling for boys and girls in both Ebiama and Amakiri has changed the expectations of those being schooled, and the expectations of their parents, as to what their future roles should *not* be: the "traditional" occupations of farming, fishing, cutting palm berries, and distilling gin. What the future should be is unclear. How to grow up in a society in which the future is seen as precarious and unknown is the issue before them.

Although our generalizations about Nigeria are limited, a case study is always potentially of broad scope. At its extreme reach, no matter how few in number, the groups under study are examples of human variability and with due caution can be used to test hypotheses or propositions. To a limited extent, the similarities and differences between the two communities afford a middle-range examination of the interrelationship of social and cultural variables as found in the spectrum of Ijo social life that falls, on the one hand, between high and low acculturated communities, and, on the other hand, between communities within a common cultural and historical framework.

In writing about change, it is difficult to avoid the implication that there was a stable time in the past, a "traditional culture," to which the present time can be compared. A more accurate view of culture is to see it as in a constant state of construction and reconstruction. The rise and fall of city-states in the eastern part of the Niger Delta (Jones 1963; Horton 1962) is a case in point. Another is the initiation and then disuse of a rite of passage in Ebiama, which is remembered only as an event when boys used to cut down their first bunch of palm berries. When we mention "tradition" we try consistently to refer to the Ijo view of their own past, some of which must be considered as a history with little supporting evidence other than the memories of the elders who provide it, and to the Ijo view of the continuation of the past to the present, 1982, the time of our restudy.

When we write of a changing culture, our description entails more than a catalog of before and after. We are particularly concerned with the concepts of autonomy and independence, as they are manifested in Ijo culture, and with the transformation of adolescents into adults. In Western society we tend to view this transformation as one from dependency to independence and autonomy. Is the same true for Ijo youth, who, as we mentioned above, are participants in a social economy that seems to be moving in the opposite direction?

■ 1
The Two Communities

FIRST IMPRESSIONS

The two Ijo communities described in this study, Ebiama and Amakiri, are located only thirty-five miles from each other, as measured by a straight line on a map, but the winding waterways of the Niger Delta increase the distance. At first sight the two towns appear similar. The average house is rectangular in shape and built of mud or cement block walls with a roof made of corrugated metal sheets, although several thatch-roofed houses are still to be found in Ebiama. The houses are close together, nestled on the riverbanks. On closer examination, however, there are dramatic differences between the two communities. Amakiri is a bustling trade town with a large marketplace, a modern bank, shops, a hospital, two secondary schools, churches, and a multiethnic population, including European engineers who have resided there during the construction of a bridge across the Forcados. Amakiri appears to be a modernized version of what Ebiama will or might become. This is a tempting vision because it offers the possibility of analyzing the changes in Amakiri from a "traditional" baseline provided by Ebiama. Time, however, obviously has not stood still in Ebiama, and its own historical and environmental conditions give it its own unique configuration. In this chapter we compare the two communities as landscapes within which to view the youths.

8

Amakiri has a population of approximately 7,000 people, large compared to most Ijo villages, and almost five times the size of Ebiama (population 1,500). Amakiri is located on the west bank of the Forcados River in Bendel state. The Forcados is a main subdivision of the Niger River in the delta. At Amakiri the river takes a wide swing, and the view from the riverbank looking downstream extends almost as far as the eye can see to the distant palm trees on the horizon. The creek on which Ebiama is found connects to the Nun River, another main subdivision of the Niger, in Rivers state. At Ebiama the horizon is nearby, trees encircle the village, and the creek is no more than a hundred yards across.

Seen from the air, the delta is a dense tropical forest, laced with rivers and punctuated by settlements on the riverbanks. Three physical zones are apparent. A narrow sandy beach area forms the apron of the delta as it meets the Atlantic Ocean. Behind this zone lies the saltwater swamp. The mangrove trees here form a close-knit canopy, almost hiding the waterways. The third and largest zone is the freshwater area, where the elevation of the land along the banks of the rivers begins to rise, affording tracts for farming. Fishing was the main occupation for men and women living in the two saltwater zones; farming, fishing, and processing of palm tree products occupied the Ijo living in the freshwater area. Both Ebiama and Amakiri are located within this latter zone.

Traveling through the delta offers another view. In this approach the delta is a mass of islands, usually with several communities on each one. During the dry season, pathways may connect the villages on the same island, but water transport is necessary to travel within the delta, except where roads and bridges have recently been built. In the early 1970s Amakiri was connected to the mainland with a roadway as part of an east-west highway that will connect Lagos to Port Harcourt. The bridge being built across the Forcados at Amakiri at the time of our study is to be a vital link in the project. (The bridge was completed and opened to traffic in 1984.)

Being located a few degrees above the equator, the towns have a typical tropical climate composed of two main seasons: a dry, humid one from November to March, and a rainy one from April to October. The length of the seasons and their intensity are approximate, although it is always very hot during the dry season. Flooding occurs toward the end of the rainy season. At Amakiri where the riverbank is almost twenty feet high during the dry season, the principal effect of the floods over the years has been to erode the riverbank. To counter-act the erosion, in the 1970s the federal government funded a landfill project that has created a large sand beach between the town and the river. At Ebiama, where the bank is half the height of Amakiri's, the river occasionally breaches the riverbank in especially rainy years, but this possibility has been much reduced since the construction of a dam across the Niger on the Benue Plateau in the early 1960s.

BACKGROUND

The Ijo (also referred to as Ijaw and Izon) population counted in the 1963 census was 1.061 million. Prior to independence in 1960, their principal area of residence in the Niger Delta was divided between the Eastern and Western regions. The boundary line was continued through subsequent subdivisions of the country into states. By 1982, the Ijo living to the east of the boundary are found largely in Rivers state, and those to the west are in Bendel state.

Ijo, both as a language and as an ethnic category, is character-ized by a range of similarities and differences. On the one hand, similarities among Ijo appear to derive from a common origin, from continuing contacts between groups, and from similar experiences with environmental conditions. In one sense this means they trace their ancestry to an eponymous founder who they believe migrated to the delta at a distant time. In another sense they are Ijo because they see themselves as being more like each other than like their mainland neighbors, the Igbo, Yoruba, Urhobo, and other Nigerian populations. On the other hand, the differences among the Ijo would seem to have been generated by long periods of separation and isolation of Ijo pop-ulations from each other, the extent of contact with non-Ijo groups, and the kinds of adaptations made to dissimilar habitats. The cultural processes of change have their counterparts in the aggregation and segmentation of Ijo communities. This cyclical social process inter-connects separate villages into one and fractures one into several; a splinter group of kinsmen departs to start a new settlement on an unoccupied part of an island in the delta and through time begins the process of aggregating itself to the neighboring communities.

Ijo is a distinct language within the South-Central branch of the Niger-Congo family. Williamson estimates that the language family subdivided approximately 7000 B.P., probably as a result of migrations into the Niger Delta (1965). Dialectical variations are important markers distinguishing one group of Ijo from another. At the widest extreme, Ijo on the eastern and western edges of the delta speak mutually unintelligible dialects. Between them is a gradient that begins at the boundary of a village, where speakers say they can recognize unique dialectical variants of the language setting themselves off from neighboring villagers. The same kind of range of variation pertains to Ijo as a social and cultural category.

The Ijo living in the Niger Delta are subdivided into forty-three *ibe*. An ibe refers to a geographical location, usually named after a man who is believed to have been a son or near descendant of Ijo, and who first settled in the area. The villages in the ibe are then named for his sons. The ibe also refers to all the founder's descendants, whether or not they reside there. Even though the term is usually translated as "clan," an ibe is neither a corporate nor an exogamous descent group. Descent is reckoned through males and females, and ibe typically were endogamous, except for a particular type of marriage, called "big dowry," usually to a non-Ijo woman. Ibe range in population from a few thousand to several hundred thousand people. Another typical feature of the ibe is a cult for the deity thought to have accompanied the founder of the ibe on his migration. These deities, along with beliefs about spirits of the bush and water, human spirits, and a female High God, provide a framework for explaining life's exigencies.

On the basis of oral histories, and linguistic and cultural evidence, Alagoa (1972) classified the ibe into three broad geographical groups: the Western, the Central, and the Eastern Delta. In the Eastern Delta the ibe developed into state organizations, while in the other areas the lineage and the village were the effective political units. They were the largest viable historical and political groupings until British colonial administration became effective at the turn of the century. There was no overarching connection among the ibe that unified the Ijo people. Ebiama and Amakiri are in the Central and Western categories, respectively.

EBIAMA

Unlike a few of the other villages in the ibe whose members find employment from nearby oil fields, Ebiama does not directly benefit from the oil industry. The indirect effects of oil income, however, in the form of government development projects and of wage income from the private and public sectors, are overwhelmingly apparent. A secondary school was initiated in 1980, a police station at approximately the same time, and a health dispensary has been in and out of operation for a few years. Market stalls had been built in the center of the village, but they were not used, nor were there marketplaces in any of the surrounding ibe villages. By the end of 1982 a new marketplace was being constructed at the north end of the village, where the government two years earlier had begun a large oil palm plantation.

Travel and communication also illustrate the magnitude of the changes. Prior to independence and a burgeoning national budget based on oil profits, Ebiama was difficult to visit. There were no roads into the delta; most transportation was by hand-paddled canoes. A few outboard engines were being used but they were low horsepower. Travel was slow and uncertain. To travel from Port Harcourt, the nearest city, located on the eastern border of the delta, took two to three days. By 1982 a road had been constructed to Yenagoa, midway to the north-central part of the delta. From there high-powered speed boats travel daily to Ebiama, reducing the total time of the journey to less than half a day from Port Harcourt. More engine-powered boats pass by Ebiama in a month than had passed by in a year two decades earlier. Concomitant with this speed and reliability of travel was the utilization of several means of communication. News comes daily by word of mouth, and passengers may also arrive with a copy of one of Nigeria's daily newspapers. Periodically a boat-library visits. Sponsored by the state government, it carries a large number of books which are loaned to readers until the boat returns several months later. Whereas prior to independence there had been only one or two radios in the village, now there are many more, as well as three television sets.

A large generator has been delivered by the government and will eventually provide electricity for the whole village. Until then about a half-dozen individuals own their own generators and use them for lights, radios, record players, television, and loudspeaker equipment. At the few outdoor lights in front of houses or shops, children gather nightly to tell stories and play games, which usually involve singing and dancing. The music heard in Ebiama is loud and has an international beat to it. Radios, phonographs, and tape recorders blare out "Congo," "Hi-life," and Bob Marley singing reggae songs, as well as records by professional Ijo music groups playing "disco." Two bands in Ebiama play disco-type music, and their amplification system and speakers allow them to be heard throughout the village.

On approaching the village a television antenna is only one of the visible indications of change in recent times. On the right a portion of the forest has been cleared, and a tractor is stationed under a corrugated metal-roof portico. The section of the village located on the left bank appears to be the same size as when I had first seen it in 1958, but the main section along the right bank has been extended to close to half a mile in length. The village has also expanded toward the forest. Whereas there had been one main path on each side of the river, two additional paths have been laid out in the main section. The second, or middle, path was constructed in 1972, about the same time the original path was widened and straightened. These are parallel to the original path and connected to it by narrow passageways between the houses. None of the paths is paved, but one man has imported a motorcycle, and there are a few bicycles in the village.

Several houses illustrate the traditional mode of construction: single story with mud walls and thatch roofs. The vast majority now have roofs of metal, and some have cement block walls. A two-story building is in use and another is under construction. Manufactured furniture and glass windows are now in common use. In this overview of the physical form of Ebiama, two constructions stand out that are of particular significance for our concern with adolescence and that portend fundamental changes for present and future generations. One is the secondary school, built on land behind the northern part of the village. The other is an uncompleted church, located in the center of the town, whose walls rise as high as the new two-story building next to it.

Without written records or archaeological evidence, the date of the founding of Ebiama is difficult to estimate. The sketchy picture we have of these early times before the paramountcy of the eastern Ijo states was replaced by British rule in 1900 rests on surmises made from present-day population distributions and the oral histories that have been passed on from previous generations. If we use geneologies, it appears that the site has been occupied since at least the early 1700s. Linguistic analysis, as previously mentioned, gives a much greater time depth to Ijo immigration into the delta. Linguistic divisions within Ijo whereby there is mutual unintelligibility between east and west segments of the population also signify a long period of residence in the delta.

Of particular historical significance to Ebiama are the Ijo found to the south and east. Referred to as Nembe, Kalabari, Okrika, and Bonny, they are city-states that developed in response to the slave trade and then to the trade in palm oil (Dike 1956; Jones 1963). Initially these were fishing villages, but their locations in the mangrove and coastal strips of the delta afforded them excellent positions to act as middlemen to European traders (Horton 1969). The effect of these trading relations was to isolate the interior delta villages from direct contact with foreign influences.

Isolation was encouraged intrasocially too because the hierarchies in the eastern states were the exceptions to the typically acephalous political communities found elsewhere. Consequently boundaries within which peaceful relations were expected were often coincident with the village limits. Travel was dangerous because of the possibility of being captured as a slave or being killed as part of a feud. The dangers of traveling, however, did not inhibit the formation of new settlements. Feuds occurred between and within families, as evidenced by the oral histories of many communities. Alagoa's history of the Ijo discloses village histories as typically referring to brothers fighting over the distribution of meat obtained in a hunt and subsequently one of them migrating to found his own family village elsewhere (Alagoa 1972).

Village units were coincident, for the most part, with extended families; political leadership coincided with leadership of war parties. Age and sex were the primary criteria for social status and the division of labor. In farming and fishing, men and women carried out separate, but cooperative activities. Men also produced palm oil and wine, carved canoes and hunted, while women were primarily responsible for cooking and rearing children. Extended families, consisting of several households of men, their wives, and children, connected to each other by common descent, could provide most of their needs. Trading for cloth, guns, machetes, and salt supplied the rest. The independence of communities and the self-sufficiency of the extended family were tempered by intermarriage and other villages and by shared beliefs in the power of local water and bush deities, called *oru*. Propitients came from within and beyond village confines to gain an oru's protection and assistance.

Once the British effected administrative control of southern Nigeria in the early 1900s, the regional linkages became emphasized and could be exercised in safety under the Pax Britannica. Since there were no official "traditional" rulers in the central Ijo area, the British designed a system of clans and an order of chiefs. The Ijo notion of ibe, referring to all descendants of a common ancestor, was used as the prototype for clans. An essential similarity between the two is that residence in the clan-ibe area presumes descent unless otherwise specified. We can see this system illustrated in the case of Opuama. Opuama, considered an ibe, consists of all the descendants of Opu, regardless of where they live. In addition, the ibe is referred to by the names of the villages thought to have been founded by the sons of Opu. The term clan, however, determines a regional unit of government; whether all the villages in the unit share equal, legitimate claims on the eponymous ancestor of the clan is beside the point. In Opuama clan there are six villages, and their historical connections are, in fact, of present-day interest. At issue is the claim that Ebiama entered the region, perhaps from Amakiri, and joined the ibe over a period of generations through the processes of intermarriage and cultural assimilation. Those who press this opinion would like to see Ebiama's claim to certain disputed lands rejected.

This dispute is instructive for two reasons. First, in the chapters that follow, references to history do not infer an unchanging or undisputed view of a past, which, at best, is described with great room for error. Second, although a court case may appear to have little interest for adolescents since it is a recounting of historically based animosities, the conflict provides an ongoing legitimization of a "we-they" attitude. The same is true of Amakiri, where a dispute over the geneology and therefore residence of the head of the clan resulted in a near blockade of Amakiri in 1982 by a neighboring village. In everyday affairs this attitude is activated in the competition for scarce resources to obtain or be the first to obtain the regional secondary school, health clinic, market stalls, police station, and so on. The isolation of communities may have subsided with colonial control, but the Ijo emphasis on village independence did not.

Up to October 1960 with the independence of Nigeria, innovations appear to have been introduced into Ebiama fairly slowly. Elderly people recall what the village was like in their youth. Apart from schoolteachers, few foreigners—meaning those not born in or married to Ebiama—had ever come to live there, and communication to the mainland was slow. Transport boats motored by slow outboard engines could be joined at the Nun River, three hours paddling away. Almost everyone had a canoe; a few individuals had their own engines.

A Nembe missionary of the Niger Delta Pastorate church

(derived from and later to be rejoined with the Christian Missionary Society) came to the village around 1910. The welcome, as later recalled, was directly related to the desire to have a school. The first primary class began in 1912. Classes were added periodically, but it was not until 1958 that the primary school of six classes was completed. Those who wished to complete primary school prior to that date had to travel to distant villages and reside there during the school sessions. They usually went on to be schoolteachers, either in Ebiama or in other Ijo communities. Few males, and many fewer females, had ventured to secondary school.

Continuing with our reference to the pre-1960s, the principal occupations were palm oil producing and "gin" distilling for the men, and farming and fishing for the women. The male occupations utilized two types of palm trees growing in the area. The palm oil tree, found in the forest, produces palm berries, which the men cut down, mash, and boil to obtain palm oil. The oil was used for household consumption in cooking or was sold at markets elsewhere. The kernels were taken to a purchasing agent of a British company, located on the Nun River. The second type of palm tree, the palm wine tree, is found in the swamps; it was tapped for palm wine and then the wine was distilled into a clear, potent alcohol called "gin" (P. Leis 1964b). In contrast to the "traditional" palm-oil-producing activity, as it is now considered by Ijo reflecting on the past, gin distilling was recognized as a new endeavor, one introduced in the 1930s by a man who had learned the procedure on a trip to the Gold Coast (now Ghana).

The gin was consumed locally or smuggled to the mainland for illegal sale. Another major activity engaging men was fishing. In this case, they would travel to other rivers, usually in the Calabar or Cameroun area, and take up residence there for years at a time. It is not unusual to find men, their wives, and children who had experienced these excursions, but the cultural impact seems minimal. The population of the fishing villages was usually all Ijo, and the working ventures were interrupted at least once a year to return to Ebiama. Women used different implements and fished differently than men. In Ebiama, women provided the daily catch, and fish was considered the essential item in the diet. Smoking fish was the method used for carrying surplus to times when fish were not available.

The staples from the farm were plantain and manioc, which the women supplemented with plantings of sugarcane, peppers, and co-

coyam. Men helped clear farmland by cutting down trees. Similarly wives helped their husbands boil the palm berries and tend the fire for distilling the palm wine. In all these activities wives were helped by their children as soon as they were old enough to participate. Not the least important way was for a boy or girl, as young as eight or nine, to care for a younger sibling to allow the mother to work. As in precolonial times, the household was able to subsist largely as a self-contained unit. There was sufficient food production to supply the daily needs. Surpluses could be exchanged for a few items made by specialists, such as canoes, climbing ropes, fishing baskets and nets, woven thatch for roofs, and so on. These same items also could be sold in distant markets. Money was needed for school fees, clothes for school, and for a number of imported items: machetes, kerosene for lamps, clothes, and medicine. Cash was also required for bridewealth and for paying the considerable costs of various kinds of ceremonial occasions. For the most part, men were expected to supply the money for the household through their occupations, while women and children supplied the foodstuffs.

By 1982 the household had lost much of its self-sufficiency and had become much more dependent on purchased basic necessities. Nowhere was this more evident than in the way fish was supplied. Whereas fresh fish had always been available daily, it had now become a rare and expensive item. Whether the decrease in supply was due to pollution of the rivers by the oil wells, the damming of the Niger River at its northern reaches, or a change in Ijo fishing techniques, fish were now being imported. Traders bringing in cartons of formerly frozen fish, referred to as "ice fish," are the principal source of fish. Coincident with this shift in the economy was the introduction of a large oil palm plantation at the north end of the village.

These examples illustrate the kinds of change that have occurred within a generation. They are both superficial and profound; they represent a new scale of cultural innovation and social relations between the community and an ever-expanding external world. These changes imply that as the population increases, communication and travel speed up, and the general standard of living improves, as evidenced by housing.

One of the paradoxes of a changing social scene such as the one we see in Ebiama is that an expanding number of life pathways may result in less rather than more freedom of choice. Ebiama appears to be turning from a mainly self-sufficient community into a dependent one. The call for daily wage laborers, especially women, promises to reduce further the possibility of households providing sufficient foodstuffs for their own needs. This paradox pertains especially to adolescents whose schooling gives them an awareness of beliefs and activities that far transcend the community boundaries. New sets of expectations for their future have the effect, however, of inhibiting them from undertaking "traditional" occupations at home.

AMAKIRI

Amakiri is laid out in the characteristic Ijo manner, with houses crowded along the riverbank, forming a long, thin stretch of about two miles. Behind the village is a dense forest, formerly uninhabited, except as the location of temporary fishing and farming sites. With increasing population pressure, however, recent inroads have been made into this area, and many of the new houses as well as government offices have been built in a cleared zone of the forest. This more modern part of the town surrounds an older part where houses are crowded close together, with kitchens, yam barns, and other storage structures in between; most of the houses have no adjacent gardens; the alleyways between structures meander in and out in a crooked fashion, often cutting across yards where children play and women cook.

The majority of the houses are built between two roads that parallel the river. The "front road" along the riverbank is a narrow, unpaved street; small stores and booths border both sides, selling foodstuffs and manufactured items and offering tailoring, shoemaking, and other services. The "back road," an extension of the highway from the town of Ughelli, is paved and runs between the town and the forest. This road is the site of heavy vehicle traffic. Trucks, minibuses, and taxis, after transporting their goods and people from the mainland towns to the Amakiri boat landing, ply along its length, looking for passengers and cargo. The boat landing located at the south end of town, or as locally known, "the Government Watersite," is the hub of the boat and car traffic. A number of services sprang up here, including a daily market for staples and manufactured goods.

The official market of Amakiri is located at the far, north end of the village, beyond which the road is not paved. This market is cyclical; it is held every twelfth day and continues for two days. The market increases the amount of traffic on the road and on the river.

People arrive the evening prior to market day and spend the night in one of the local guesthouses or camp along the road or in their boats. There is a great deal of drinking, music, and entertainment. The languages heard every day in the town include Ijo, Isoko, Urhobo, Igbo, Yoruba, English, and pidgin English. A number of Isokos and Urhobos are long-term settlers in the community. The Isoko and Urhobo, Edo speakers—a language in the same Kwa-language family as Ijo—come from a similar environment and share a number of cultural features with the Ijo (Bradbury 1957, 132). Of particular importance is their ideology of descent, which, as we see in the next chapter, complements the marriage system in Amakiri. Most Amakiri residents master at least one other language besides their native tongue. Thus, the impression one receives is of a crowded and busy trading center and transportation junction where the native inhabitants are in contact with a number of visitors in a variety of capacities. These have been characteristic features of Amakiri for some time, due in large part to its location and history. Many recent developments, however, have further created a busy village community.

According to Alagoa (1972), the Western Delta area has been settled by its Ijo population at least since the close of the fifteenth century when Portuguese explorers observed "all territory east of the Forcados River occupied by 'Jos'" (1972, 59). They lived in a densely populated area and produced "canoes made of a single trunk."

Amakiri is one of twelve towns of the Torowei ibe. Unlike most other Ijo ibe, which recognize a principle of ambilineal descent for choosing to reside with the father's or mother's kinsmen, the village units of Torowei are based almost exclusively on patrilineal descent. The majority of the Toro towns lie along both sides of the Forcados, where various sections of the ibe gradually moved from a more western location along the Bolous Creek. The Toro believe that their history may be traced back to an ancestor, Okosibo, who fled Benin because of the atrocities committed by the Oba, the traditional ruler of Benin, against his people.

Leadership was vested in the descent line of one of Okosibo's sons and took the form of a *pere* (king), who resided in Amakiri. The members of Torowei ibe refer to the pereship as an important unifying symbol, even though the office had remained unfilled because of intervillage disputes over who should succeed to office. The last pere died in 1971. Currently, each Toro town has its own council of elders, but they act in unison through a common council to make decisions and set policy regulating matters of local concern such as marriage, burial, and inheritance.

Notwithstanding the office of the pere, the western Ijo, similar to Ebiama and the Ijo in the Central Delta, were politically decentralized. Village units were essentially independent, uniting occasionally with other village segments in the ibe to carry out a raid on a village in another ibe, or even in their own. The activity that brought people into contact with others beyond the limits of the village was trading for manufactured items and for salt. Apart from this, the village economy was essentially self-sufficient, based on fishing, farming, and hunting.

With British domination came political hierarchy, beginning with district officers and native courts, and continuing to the formation of a representative form of government. The British also brought Christianity. The group most active in southern Nigeria was the London-based Anglican Christian Missionary Society, a branch of which reached Amakiri in 1905. By 1906 Amakiri was the center of regional missionary activity, with a church and mission house built along the river. The mission exercised its major influence through the introduction of British-style schools, and by 1910 classes were conducted in English in the Amakiri mission building for boys in the area. A Catholic mission school opened in the 1940s.

During the first half of the twentieth century, Amakiri grew into a large town and a regional marketing center. By the 1950s Amakiri was a well-known community in the delta because of its size (2,000 people), its facilities, and its contact with other neighboring ethnic groups (N. Leis 1964). "The presence of a large market, both United Africa Company and John Holt Company 'factories,' a dispensary, a maternity center, a local court and a post-office" (p. 22) brought many non-Ijo and Ijo visitors to the community. During her study in 1959, Leis was also impressed by the heterogeneity of Amakiri, by the inhabitants' ability to speak English, and by the busy traffic along the river. However, in emphasizing these cosmopolitan features of Amakiri she was explicitly contrasting it with the relatively isolated and much smaller Ebiama.

Undoubtedly, when compared to other Ijo towns at that time, Amakiri was unique in some respects. However, as with most other Ijo communities that were without road connections to other settlements, it also was isolated from the mainland by the surrounding waterways. It was basically a horticultural society with a number of secondary occupations: fishing, trading, palm oil production, and occasional temporary employment by the men in building and transportation. The division of labor between men and women was pronounced. The women were responsible for food production, farming, and fishing. Their husbands provided the land and the fishing rights to certain fish ponds, but the men themselves did no work on the farm. Many of the women were also engaged in trading at the local market, and some of them traveled as well to markets long distances away. The men's occupations included trading, shopkeeping, hauling gravel by canoes, unloading ships, building houses, canoe making, and a number of service occupations such as tailoring and shoemaking. For decades, Amakiri men have sought employment in the cities, going as far away as Lagos and Kano. This resulted in a gradual out-migration of younger men who at an early age began to join relatives in the cities, either for schooling or for employment. The occupations abandoned by Amakiri natives have been taken up by Isokos and Urhobos.

Amakiri residents agree that the most significant development of the postindependence era was the construction of the highway or back road connecting the town to the rest of Bendel state. This project, the origin of which was a self-help collaborative effort between Amakiri and other riverine towns in 1961, was completed during the Third National Development Plan of 1970–74. The road construction presaged a number of other developments which altered the appearance of the town.

In the early 1970s Amakiri became a suboffice of the Local Government Council, headquartered in Bomadi. Because Bomadi is located on an island, many government officials prefer to reside in Amakiri and commute to their offices by boat. Consequently, government offices and low-cost housing units for minor functionaries were built in 1975. Until 1976 there were two small primary schools in the town. A secondary school was established by the Bendel state government in 1969. The more recent (1980) establishment of a girls' secondary school has further increased the number of students and teachers in town.

In the mid-1970s a hospital was built in Amakiri as part of the Bendel State Zonal Health System. The hospital provides free health care and prenatal services for both out- and in-patients. It is, however, chronically understaffed, with only one doctor and four or five nurses in residence. The hospital also shares the fate of the dispensary in that they both lack funds for medicines and vaccines.

In the late 1970s the Rural Electrification Board established a plant in Amakiri with the intention of providing electricity to the town. After a few months of operation the generator burned out and has not been repaired. Since the electrical system is not functioning, the majority of the houses use kerosene lanterns for lighting. The more affluent and the store and hotel owners have generators. Some of the larger hotels have installed bottled gas stoves. The expense of obtaining refills is beyond the means of all but a small handful of households. Most women cook on woodburning stoves or on one-burner kerosene cookers. The Water Board has provided running water to the town since 1980, which has helped eradicate a number of water-borne diseases, but most compounds have no connection to the main water line. Children are sent to fetch water at the public taps for cooking and washing dishes. Bathing and washing clothes are done in the river.

In 1980, a German-Nigerian joint enterprise secured a contract from the federal government of Nigeria to construct a bridge spanning the Forcados River between Amakiri and Sagbama on the opposite bank. The bridge is part of a new major thoroughfare, the East-West Road, connecting Lagos to Port Harcourt. It will provide one of the only crossing points on the Niger in southern Nigeria. Amakiri residents expect an unprecedented development boon after its completion.

Among other recent developments are the establishment of a commercial bakery, a fish farm, a poultry farm, and, in January 1982, a branch office of the African Continental Bank. There are also a number of guesthouses and hotels in town, the largest being the newest; it is located near the junction of the new road leading to the bridge. The town has a Postal Service Agency, operated by one elderly Amakiri man, where mail can be picked up. The facility also doubles as a book and paper store for the school. Some distance away a large air-conditioned building with its own generator contains a radio telephone system, but it is not yet operative. Besides the local government offices, the other public buildings in the town are the police station and a fairly large open shed adjacent to the Government Watersite, which is used for political meetings.

Almost all the houses are built of mud-brick and corrugated iron roofs; only a few still have thatched roofs. Houses currently under construction are made of cement blocks, with concrete floors and corrugated iron roofs, and have indoor toilets, indoor kitchens, and running water. Most of them are owned by Amakiri natives, currently resident outside of the community, who are preparing to return to their hometown for their years of retirement. The town offers little in the way of public entertainment facilities. The construction of a movie house was begun some years ago with the erection of steel girders of ambitious proportions, but then it was abandoned. Rock groups are occasionally invited to perform at one of the larger hotels. Now and then films are shown in a shed owned by one of the residents. There are, however, hundreds of battery-run cassette recorders and radios, and the shops and hotels with generators also have television sets.

Its cosmopolitan appearance notwithstanding, Amakiri remains a rural settlement, with few amenities and opportunities. With the exception of the back road, the streets and alleyways are unpaved. During the rainy season many of them are almost impassable, the mud seemingly swallowing up any amount of gravel that might be poured into it. The back road itself is so full of potholes that many commercial vehicles refuse to make the trip, or charge double from Ughelli to Amakiri.

SUMMARY

In summary, the geographical positions of Ebiama and Amakiri are important for understanding the historic circumstances that fostered communal self-sufficiency—economically, politically, and ideologically. By 1982 location had become less significant. Over twenty years of independence from British colonial rule had given Nigeria ample opportunity to incorporate the most distant and isolated communities in the delta into a national polity. The means to do so have been provided by the income from oil. As in many other parts of the world, a dramatic expansion in the range of communications and economic opportunities appears to liberate individuals from a narrow limit of life pathways. At the same time, this freedom seems vitiated by their dependency on politics and markets that operate on a level beyond individual or community control. In the next chapter we continue the description of the two communities, focusing on their cultural features. We then turn to the ways adolescents act in their present milieu and prepare themselves for the future.

■ 2
The Social Context

THE WEB OF RELATIONSHIPS

Like a pebble falling into the center of a pool of water, at birth an Ijo infant enters a proverbial web of kinship that ripples outward in ever-widening circles. Initially the significant linkages are based on residence in the household and village quarter, and on the choices a child's parents have made about strengthening or weakening particular relationships. Later in life the decisions will shift to the individual, as he or she combines individual preferences and historical happenstance with the expectations of how an Ijo should act. Although all societies have such rules, they receive either more or less explicitness in the form of "laws" and rulings by persons in positions of authority.

For the Ijo in Ebiama and Amakiri, two sets of rules coincide or, at times, collide with each other. In one set, rules are largely consensual, based on assumptions acquired during socialization, reaffirmed by living elders as the practice of the past, and enforced by beliefs in a High God who predetermines the course of human and natural events; in the authority and power of deceased elders; and in the spirits (*orumo*). In the other, the rules are part of the new social order: Nigerian laws enforced by the police, authoritative statements from political officials, from people with wealth and positions of power, and from schoolteachers and other professionals. In this chapter we describe the interweaving of social rules with social practice in social organization, economic relations, and religious convictions to provide the format for viewing the lives of Ijo youth in the 1980s.

SOCIAL ORGANIZATION

The Ijo in both Ebiama and Amakiri stress that on marrying, a woman should join her husband (a virilocal rule of residence), who should reside in his father's quarter (a patrilocal rule). In Amakiri these rules are consistent with the inheritance of rights and property through agnatic links so that a village quarter can be unambiguously defined as a patrilineal descent group. When a man pays bridewealth to his bride's family (referred to as a "small-dowry" marriage by English speakers in Amakiri), he acquires the right to incorporate the children he procreates with his wife into his descent group.

In Ebiama, bridewealth gives the man the right to have sex with his wife, and, should she commit adultery, he can claim a fine from his wife and her lover. A marriage fee, however, does not always give the husband the right to add the children of his marriage to his descent group. He can do so in one type of marriage, where his wife is acquired through "big dowry" *(fe ere)*, which is similar to the "small dowry" *(ekie ere)* in Amakiri. Although the English terminology is confusing, the Ijo terms are parallel when we see that another form of marriage once practiced in Amakiri is recalled as *fei ere*, "big dowry," the same term as in Ebiama.

To contrast the difference in the types of marriages between the two communities, it would be as though Amakiri Ijo dropped the significance between small- and big-dowry marriage in favor of the latter. The Amakiri people reflect that this probably was the case because they realize they are unique among Ijo in stressing patrilineal instead of matrilineal descent and inheritance. How recently this change, or its cause, occurred is impossible to determine. It appears to reflect the interconnected influence of contact with European ideas; marriage with neighboring peoples, the Isoko and Urhobo, who are patrilineal; and an affluence amply demonstrated in the form of permanent dwellings which give impetus to sons claiming the inheritance of the houses they grow up in. The latter, economic, factor can be seen influencing a similar change to patrilineality in Ebiama (P. Leis 1972, 17).

The small-dowry marriage in Ebiama is by far the most frequent; a smaller amount of bridewealth is paid, and inheritance is matrilineal—between between mother's brother and sister's son, and between mother and daughter. When a greater amount is paid, and such marriages only occur with non-Ijo women who are then brought to live in Ebiama, inheritance passes between father and children. Even though the emphasis on residence in both forms of marriage is patrilocal, the opportunities for residing with maternal kinsmen for children of small-dowry marriages are attractive. The residential group, then, is usually interconnected through both agnatic and uterine ties so that the quarters form what may be called ambilineal or nonunilineal descent groups.

The bridewealth in Amakiri is set at fifty naira, the major part of which is paid to the father of the bride. (In 1982 the average exchange rate for the naira was one naira = $1.60.) Smaller amounts are given to her mother, to her mother's father, and to the bride as consent fees. The total amount in Ebiama comes to one hundred naira, with the distribution similar to Amakiri, even though the bride "belongs" to her mother's brother. There is no set amount for a big-dowry wife.

There are seven quarters in Amakiri and five in Ebiama. The quarters in both towns were spatially removed from one another in the past, but as a consequence of population growth, they spread until they became contiguous, except in Ebiama where the river has kept one of the quarters separated. There are no other boundary markers to separate the quarters from one another, but all families within a quarter consider themselves closely related. They recognize a distant kinship to members of all the other quarters, but if geneological ties cannot be traced, propinquity is the main point of reference for social cohesion or conflict.

When referring to social units, we find similar extensions of meaning in the Ijo word *ware* as we do in the English usage of *family*. Literally translated, a *ware* is a house, or those who live in the house, or all those descended from the head of the household, or all those descended from the founder of the quarter or subdivisions of it. The word is understood by its context.

Members of a ware have rights to certain plots of land within the quarter. When a man contemplates marriage, he asks permission of the leaders of the ware, usually the oldest men, to erect a building close to his father's compound. To this building he brings his wife or wives, and it is here that ideally his children grow up. As we shall see, there are many exceptions to this rule. Without exception in Amakiri, however, spouses are never buried in the same location; every man and woman will be brought to his or her father's place of residence for burial. In this way a person's spirit joins with those of the deceased of the quarter. In Ebiama the place of burial will depend on where the deceased has resided the longest.

The multiple meanings of a ware, and especially the variety of choices that enter into the composition of kin groups in Ebiama, make the "household" a complex unit to define, which is not an unusual problem in comparative research on households (Netting, Wilk, and Arnould 1984). Ideally, Ijo households contain a man, his wives, and their unmarried children. Each wife is provided with her own living area, consisting of a room for sleeping and occasionally another to use as a sitting room. All the wives' rooms are adjacent to each other in a common structure and open onto a common porch area. The porch is used for eating, grinding foodstuffs, and washing dishes, and it is here that the wives and older girls spend much of their time tending the younger children. Wives also have separate kitchens, somewhat removed from the main structure. The husband has his own living area within the compound, and his own reception room where he entertains visitors. He alternates sleeping with his wives, either in his own or in the wife's bedroom. Similarly, he alternates eating meals prepared by each of his wives. The children of each mother share her sleeping quarters, moving to vacant rooms or to other compounds as they get older.

In practice there are many exceptions to this household arrangement. (See chapter 3 for a detailed description of households.) If there is no space available in her husband's compound, a woman may live with her parents or in a separate apartment. If she is divorced, a woman leaves her husband's compound and may take up residence with either her new husband, her parents, or her relatives. On divorcing, a woman usually leaves the older children with the husband and takes the younger ones with her until they mature, when they also should return to the father's residence. Thus, it is not unusual to find a household occupied by children aged nine and older, whose mothers are absent. The household composition is further complicated by the addition of children of brothers and sisters who live elsewhere but who send their children to the home village for schooling. This mobile, indeterminant character of households is typical of many African societies (Guyer 1981, 98).

A household, then, is a descriptive term that refers to a group of individuals, one of whom is recognized as the head; the others are related to him or her consanguinely or affinally. (The head of the household is most often a male. When a female is the head of household she is usually elderly and divorced or widowed.) They share the proceeds, to some extent, of their labor. They may reside in one or more houses, or two or more households may occupy one large dwelling. A "compound" refers to the physical arrangement of buildings for one or more households and can also include unrelated visitors or migrants. When there is more than one household in a compound, the heads are usually brothers or a father and son.

The difference between Amakiri's patrilineal and Ebiama's matrilateral emphasis is not as great as it might appear. On the one hand, the value placed on patrilocality in Ebiama gives sons de facto rights to the property held by their father's quarter, even though they may choose to join their mother's brothers. On the other, in Amakiri, children of the same mother share matrilateral kin affiliations and common economic interests, and thereby constitute a subgroup among the agnatically related siblings. Full siblings usually give more financial assistance to each other than to half siblings, and after their mother's death, they claim her accumulated wealth or private property, such as money, jewelry, cloth, and even buildings she has erected for her business activities. These inheritance patterns reflect the distinctions—and contradictions—between inheritance rules, marriage types, and the affective relationships formed through common residence. Because of both the high rate of migration and the availability of land, there has been little conflict thus far in either community for building lots.

Another distinction in types of marriages that has come to be increasingly recognized in recent years, especially in Amakiri, is one between "customary" and "Christian" marriages. The latter require the additional step of a church ceremony. Christian marriages may be polygynous, with a man marrying his first wife in church and several subsequent ones in "customary" union. Both of these forms are recognized as equally binding and respectable as long as the bridewealth is paid. While the Anglican church tries to discourage polygynous unions, it does not openly object to them, especially in places such as Amakiri where the majority of its staunchest supporters are polygynously married.

Marriage in Ebiama and Amakiri is most frequently polygynous. Even though acquiring additional wives is not considered an expensive proposition, the conflicts engendered by jealousy and the necessity of treating each subhousehold unit equally appear to inhibit the stability of large numbers of multiple marriages. Those husbands with more than two wives are politically astute, at least in their domestic spheres of influence. They are usually considered wealthy too, since women do the farming and provide for the everyday needs of the children. Furthermore, children represent potential wealth, as well as additional labor, because the Ijo perceive of inheritance as flowing from sons to fathers as readily as the reverse. Men believe that having many wives and therefore many children is one way to achieve economic success and social esteem.

Until recently the quarters were exogamous, since individuals felt that potential partners within the same quarter were "too closely related" to marry, even when the kin ties could not be traced. Preferred marriage partners were members of another quarter, of another town in the ibe, or of another Ijo ibe, in that order of preference. Nevertheless, Amakiri men will marry Isoko and Urhobo women because they too are organized patrilineally. Ebiama men wishing to obtain a big-dowry wife had to marry afar, usually an Igbo, since local Ijo women would not be allowed to enter into this type of marriage. To remove a daughter's children from the matrilineal line of inheritance would be, for those in Ebiama, similar to placing her in the category of slave. Marriages now occur between members of the same quarter when elders find it difficult to trace the specific geneological connections between the two.

Divorce is relatively easy and frequent. Most often women will initiate the divorce, invariably so if they do not become pregnant and believe it is their husband's fault. Women will also divorce if their husband treats them badly by not sharing his time and gifts equally among them.

Widows are inherited in accordance with the agnatic and uterine principles discussed previously. In Amakiri, widows are supposed to marry one of the deceased's brothers or sons who is older than the woman in question. In Ebiama the same is true in the case of a big-dowry wife; a small-dowry wife would be expected to marry the brother, mother's brother, or sister's son of her spouse. Frequently, however, women prefer to return to their own natal villages and live with a brother or sister or in their father's compound. This is especially true for older women who have no sons and are no longer of childbearing age.

Social differentiation has shifted from being primarily based on age, sex, and number of descendants to one also influenced by education and occupation. In Amakiri, distinctions based on wealth and power are more clearly visible than in Ebiama, where an egalitarian ethic remains in effect despite differences that are beginning to appear in types of housing and in other expenditures such as the purchase of speed boats and the expenses of a burial. In Amakiri a number of families have managed to achieve higher status by sending sons to secondary and postsecondary schools, or into business or politics, which resulted in prestigious, high-paying jobs. Among these successful sons are three elected representatives to the state and the federal government, whose display of wealth and power clearly places them into a separate category, along with dentists, lawyers, school principals, and doctors who have built spacious houses in the community where they return for the holidays and for the town festival. The addition of a number of migrant professionals—schoolteachers, nurses, doctors, and engineers—has resulted in the emergence of a small middle class.

ECONOMY

Horticulture is the primary source of subsistence in both Ebiama and Amakiri, an occupation almost exclusively the domain of women. The women also used to provide fish when it was more readily available. In Amakiri, women are also heavily engaged in marketing, whereas the absence of a local market in the Ebiama area eliminates this activity except for the few who travel to distant markets. Men help cut down trees to prepare a new area for planting, but their primary occupations have shifted through time.

Most of the farms lie along the river, and the farming cycle is dependent on the annual flooding of the delta rivers and creeks. The water levels begin to rise in June, reach a crest in late October, and then steadily subside until January. During the flood period, the farms on the low side of the river bends are covered by water, limiting their use but making them especially fertile. Farmland is plentiful, and if a woman finds she needs land, as is often the case with the Isoko and Urhobo in Amakiri, she can rent land from one of the quarters.

The farming cycle begins in late January, when the land is cleared and tilled. In early February, pepper, groundnuts, cassava, and sugar-cane are planted at the water's edge. Later in the month, yams, plantain, and cocoyams are planted somewhat farther inland. Yams are tended and weeded throughout the dry season. Harvesting of yams and of most other crops is done before the flooding starts again. Plantains and cassava, however, may be harvested throughout the year since they are planted above the high water level. Ebiama and Amakiri women use most of their crops for their households; the latter usually have a surplus, however, which they sell.

No day's diet is complete without fish. Women used to be able to supply their household needs, but as mentioned previously, frozen fish is now being imported. Fishing is not an everyday activity for most women, and some women do not fish at all. During the dry season, the fishing is done by nets in the river or in the ponds found in the forests. Most of the fishing is day fishing; a woman alone or with one or two others leaves early in the morning and returns in the late afternoon. Shrimping during the rainy season takes longer since several days are required to set up traps and then collect the catch.

In addition to farming and fishing, most Amakiri women as a matter of course are involved in marketing and trading. For the most part, these activities are dependent on the other two occupations and involve the selling of foodstuffs grown by the woman herself. A number of women also buy and sell produce grown by others, or items, such as cloth or pots, made by others. Trading is thus either part time or full time. The latter involves taking wares to markets outside of the town, sometimes as far as Onitsha or Warri. A few women, who are not primarily involved in farming and fishing, work as seamstresses, shopkeepers, or schoolteachers.

In Ebiama, women also find daily wage employment at the nearby oil palm plantation. The plantation, since it has only recently been developed, has had small economic impact on the community, but its implications for the future are far-reaching. The Nigerian government's aim, aside from increasing palm oil production, is to provide an incentive to the rural population to remain at home rather than to migrate to the cities. At the same time, such actions create a precarious economy by inducing women to give up their farming and fishing for home consumption in order to receive an unsteady wage income from the plantation, when and if the opportunity arises.

The majority of the non-food-producing occupations are filled by males. These men may be divided into two sectors: (1) those who are self-employed, and (2) those who are daily wage earners or are on professional contracts. These sectors represent not only a division of labor but also a shift from the past, when most men worked individually or in cooperative groups as palm oil producers, gin distillers, or canoe carvers, to the present-day emphasis on service occupations and wage-earning tasks. In the first sector we currently find barbers, carpenters, shoemakers, and tailors. Also included in this sector are small-scale business entrepreneurs: bakers, transporters, builders, and owners of hotels, restaurants, beer parlors, or small shops. Jobs in the second sector include block moulders, gravel diggers, and plantation workers. Many individuals are active in both sectors. One may own a shop, but also haul gravel; another may operate a speed boat, work as a laborer in block moulding, and also run a beer parlor, and so on.

While the numbers and types of occupations have increased during the past years, many men still look for employment in the cities. They may do so for a relatively short period of time, save money to set up business or to build a house, and then return. Others stay longer, only returning to the community when they are ready to retire. For the young people of the town there are few employment opportunities. This is especially true for those who have completed the secondary school and do not wish to continue in their fathers' footsteps. Out-migration for females as well as males has begun now that girls are completing their schooling and searching for employment.

RELIGION

The majority of people in Amakiri and Ebiama think of themselves as Christian, which they see as consistent with the native belief in a single High God. The rest believe in the power of a number of local deities. There are no cult houses or cult groups dedicated to the worship of the High God. Although she is a distant figure, she is the ultimate explanation for all worldly events. Of concern in helping to understand the vageries of everyday life are beliefs in the local deities, ancestors, and witches (P. Leis 1964a). Cult houses for local water and forest spirits are located along Amakiri's "front" road. In Ebiama all the cult houses had been destroyed or abandoned when we arrived early in 1982, but one was restored during the course of the year.

The Ijo in Amakiri have small shrines for their ancestors in the compounds where they lived during their lifetimes. In Ebiama, appeals to an ancestor are performed in front of the deceased's last dwelling. The dead are asked to protect their descendants from witches and to help the living prosper and bear children. The dead may also cause illness or harm if they are offended by certain kinds of transgressions, such as adultery, or if a menstruating woman touches the food she serves to her husband.

Christianity came to Amakiri in 1906 and to Ebiama at approximately the same time via the Christian Missionary Society of London. In Amakiri, St. Matthew's Anglican ministry is still the largest in the community and the seat of a regional subdivision of the Anglican Archdeaconry, serving a large area in both Rivers and Bendel states. The Anglican church in the past few years has been losing popularity to a revivalist group, the Cherubim and Seraphim. There is also a Catholic, a Seventh-Day Adventist, and a Jehovah's Witnesses church, each with a relatively small following. The Cherubim and Seraphim have also established a small church in Ebiama, and there are other small Christian sects, but the majority of Christians are Anglicans.

Christians and non-Christians alike believe in the power of witches. While there are supposed to be both good and bad witches, they are mostly considered a possible explanation for infertility, for children's illness or death, and for all sorts of misfortunes in adult life. People may become witches without being aware of it and thus do ill to others unwittingly. Diviners, who also form the interpretive link between the living and the spirits and ancestors, help determine whether somebody is a witch, but no cure exists for ridding oneself of this affliction.

It may be said that the religious life of the two communities receives its fullest expression in dramatically similar and different ways. The similarity lies in the extended funerals given to individuals with two or more generations of descendants. It is a time when the extensive and interdependent social ties of the living and the dead are reaffirmed. The difference is found in an annual festival in Amakiri, called *seigbein*, which is absent in Ebiama. The seigbein is celebrated in March or April, depending on the correspondence between the appearance of the new moon and the next scheduled market day. The spring festival is said to serve the dual purpose of cleansing the town of sins and wrong deeds, and of rededicating it to the ancestors. An important part of the festival is the ceremonial dance held by newly circumcised women, which we describe in chapter 4. Women never receive a clitoridectomy in Ebiama, which may partly account for the absence of the festival there. The patrilineal emphasis in Amakiri also provides an ancestral following that is more clearly coincident with the totality of the town than is the case in Ebiama.

■ 3
Households and the PSU

METHODOLOGY

For the study of adolescent life in Ebiama and Amakiri we selected sections of each community that satisfy the criteria of a Primary Social Unit (PSU). Whiting, Child, and Lambert define a PSU as "a small group of families setting themselves off from a large society by some social factor in such a way that: (1) they conceive of themselves as some sort of unit, (2) they have frequent interaction, and (3) they possess temporal and/or spatial stability" (1966, 23). The concept is useful for comparing societies of different sizes and for focusing on the noninstitutional aspects of socialization practices. Previous studies of child rearing have used various criteria for determining the nature and the boundaries of the PSU. These ranged from fenced cattle kraals, clan neighborhoods, and ethnic groups within a larger settlement to local groups demarcated by criteria of caste or religion. Village quarters (ware) in both Ebiama and Amakiri met the criteria for a PSU, although there are certain qualifications that will be mentioned later.

In addition to the three criteria, the Harvard Adolescent Project members determined the PSUs should be chosen with consideration to the number of subjects available in certain age-groups. The average age of menarche would be a benchmark for drawing a sample that would encompass the prepuberty and postpuberty age periods, which we estimated to be five years on each side of the age of menarche. Since boys mature on the average two years later than girls, we added two years to the girls' age of menarche and from that age drew the male youth population at five plus and minus years. In the Ijo case, the age of menarche is estimated to be around fourteen years, which meant that our sample for girls would be drawn between the ages of nine and nineteen, and for boys between eleven and twenty-one.

We planned to select approximately four males and females at each age level; we refer to this group as the "general" sample. From this number we would then select a smaller number, the "long interview" sample, for repeated observation, lengthy interviews, and cognitive testing. A still smaller number would comprise our "intensive interview" sample. The numbers chosen were thought to be adequate, but they were also picked because it seemed unlikely we could fulfill our interviewing and observational objectives in the time available with a greater number.

Finally, we agreed that we would weigh and measure each subject in the general sample twice, as near to the beginning and to the end of our field studies as possible. The relative height gains during this period, in addition to whatever physiological growth observations could be made, would enable us to place each individual into pre-growth-spurt, growth spurt, and post-growth-spurt periods.

A major difficulty, especially in Ebiama, of pursuing these objectives was the determination of age. In Amakiri, birth dates were recorded more often than not, and individuals readily knew their birthdays. This was not true in Ebiama. Relative age is stressed, although not always agreed on, but dates of birth were recorded for relatively few individuals. A census we took in 1958 enabled us to fix the birth dates of those in their midtwenties. The task for us was to take those with known birth dates, either because they were recorded or clearly associated with a historic event, and sort them by the relative ages recognized by individuals. The Ijo have a term for age-mates, *ogbo*, referring to those born at the same time, but the duration of the "same time" is never fixed. Even though the Ijo did not express a value for any particular size of age-group, we surmised that if a large number of infants born near in time to each other survived, the time period would be as short as a few days or a month. If the survival rate was low then the time span might be increased. Whatever historical functions the ogbo may have had, they persist mainly as a set of joking relationships, a sharp contrast to the expected deferential behavior of younger to older persons. The estimation of age was complicated by still two other factors. One concerns lack of knowledge because of being born elsewhere. A woman marrying into the village, for example, is hard pressed to judge her age relative to others. The other factor is height. Taller youngsters tend to be perceived and to perceive themselves as older than their shorter cohorts. Students in the secondary school in Ebiama communicated this perception clearly in response to our request that they line themselves up according to their relative ages: each was to stand to the left of a person younger than himself or herself. The line turned out to be an almost perfect gradation in height from shortest to tallest. We mention these difficulties by way of offering a cautionary note to approaching what is usually thought to be the objective fact of age. Just as the biological fact of menarche varies between individuals and between average age at menarche in groups for a number of reasons, so too the perception of age can have a latitude that varies with more conditions than the date of birth alone.

We emphasize, therefore, that our references to specific chronological age periods in the chapters that follow are primarily derived from our own perceptions and deductions, based on extended observations of who is doing, or expected to be doing, certain activities.

Once the PSUs were selected and the adolescent population was identified, the quarters were mapped and a household survey was made of the adolescents' residences. Participant observation of the PSU proceeded throughout the research period, with the adolescent population as its focus. Informal interviews were also conducted with the parents and older siblings of the sample.

A number of formal interviews and psychological measures were administered to two different subsamples of the general sample (or total population) of subjects.

The "long interview" sample consisted of approximately half of the subjects in the general sample, chosen so that approximately equal numbers of males and females were included at each age and with the highest number of subjects concentrated in the circumpubertal age-groups (ages twelve to sixteen). These youngsters were administered a lengthy interview in which they were asked to describe their daily routine, their relationship to their parents, siblings, and friends, and finally to talk about their plans and aspirations. They were also subjects of routine as well as scheduled spot observations.

In addition, everyone in the group was administered the draw-a-person test, which was designed to examine an individual's sex-role preference. In this test, the subjects were given a piece of paper and pencil and instructed to draw a picture of a person. When they asked about the kind of person they were expected to draw, they were told that it could be any kind. When the first picture was completed, they were asked to draw the opposite-sex person and to number the two drawings. After the two pictures were completed, we asked a number of questions regarding the sex and age of the person drawn, if she or he was real or imagined, and in what activity he or she was engaged. The primary concern in administering this measure was noting which sex was drawn first and the degree of sexual differentiation between male and female drawings.

The same sample of subjects was also administered a number of cognitive developmental measures, including a moral dilemma and a test of formal operations. The findings on these measures are not discussed in the present volume, but may be found elsewhere (Hollos, Leis, and Turiel 1986; Hollos and Richards 1988).

The "intensive interview" sample consisted of our key informants among the youth. We came to know these individuals best, and toward the end of the research period we felt free to discuss most topics with many of them, except their sexual experiences, which only the boys would comment on.

This group was administered the magic man interview, which is an examination of occupational and family-role preferences. The youngsters were asked to pretend that a magician came to town who gave them a number of choices about what they could be. They were also asked to state their preference for one of a paired set of identities. The identities were mother, father, girl, boy, and infant. The sex of the infant was not specified. A total of six paired choices were given, allowing each informant to choose between various ages and sexes. These pairs included mother or father, girl or boy, girl or infant, boy or infant, girl or mother, boy or father. Finally, the subjects were asked whether in their next life they would like to be reborn as a boy or a girl.

The young people's further ideas about others as male and female beings in their society were elicited with the help of intensive semantic interviews. This interview was based on the assignment of personality descriptors, commonly used in the Ijo language, to one of the sexes. In Amakiri the terms were originally elicited from another group of informants who were asked to describe the behavior of a bad/good man, woman, or child. The resulting thirty-five terms were written on three-by-five-inch file cards and presented individually to our subjects. They were asked whether the particular term described the behavior or was more characteristic of males or females or both. In Ebiama, informants were asked to describe themselves, and we then compared these self-descriptors according to gender. We also asked each respondent which of five frequently used descriptors applied to both or either sex.

Toward the end of the research period an intensive interview on gender identity and sexual practices was conducted with a smaller number of boys and girls from this sample. By this time the youngsters were familiar with the researchers and their assistants and seemed comfortable with the interview situation. In Amakiri, the boys were interviewed by an Ijo male assistant without the presence of M. Hollos, and the sessions were tape-recorded. These recordings were subsequently transcribed and discussed. The girls' interviews transpired in the presence of Hollos and her female assistant, who explained the questions when necessary to the girls. In Ebiama, girls were interviewed by L. Kossin, the female research associate, aided by an Ijo female assistant. P. Leis interviewed the Ebiama boys with the aid of an Ijo male assistant.

THE PSU IN EBIAMA

Two adjacent quarters, Siba and Osigiri, were selected for the PSU in Ebiama. While they were similar to the other quarters in most respects, their initial appeal rested on their central location and on the access offered by our assistants living there. Just as the quarters imperceptibly blend into each other, so too, we should emphasize, do the social boundaries of the PSU blend into other social units. The quarter in which one lives is important for a number of reasons, but ties of kinship and friendship extend to all parts of the village and beyond. As we shall see, one of the striking implications of the high divorce rates, coupled with an emphasis on bilateral kinship, is the migratory life histories of individuals as they move among households and live with a variety of kinsmen.

Osigiri is marked by several distinguishing factors. It is the home of the *amayanabo* ("chief") of the village; it has the only two-story buildings, but they do not belong to the chief; and it is the location of a partially constructed church. All of these might indicate that Osigiri has a richer or more elite population than the other quarters, but each of the other quarters also has features representing wealth or prominence. Siba owns a great deal of land in and around the village, including the large tract just south of Ebiama which the quarter provided for the construction of the primary school. The priest for the cult of a renowned spirit, named Kelele, lives in Siba. In the other three quarters we find individuals with television sets; a businessman with a high-powered motor boat; a government official building a modern house, equipped with indoor plumbing and running water, to be ready when he retires from his job in Lagos; and so on. Apart from these variations in individual roles and representation of wealth, Osigiri and Siba are indistinguishable from the other quarters and therefore may be considered representative of them.

The similarity of Ebiama quarters to each other is emphasized in the extension of kin and affinal ties throughout the community. This interlinkage is important to consider when applying the criteria of a PSU to the social reality of a quarter. Much more so than in Amakiri with its coincidence of patrilineality and patrilocality, and with its greater incidence of interethnic marriages, in Ebiama individuals are linked significantly through both parents and through both sets of grandparents virtually to every quarter. This means that when a young person moves out of a household, he or she can associate with kin in other quarters as easily as in his or her own. Indeed, since the quarter is usually exogamous, if a youth's mother is from Ebiama, his ties will be stronger to her quarter in some respects than to his own. Diffused relationships also result in another modification of a PSU criterion. Although the boundaries of the quarters tend to be stable, there is frequent movement of the population across them. Daily visiting is one type of movement, but there are much more permanent moves as children are moved to new residences, both within and outside of Ebiama, as a result of their parents divorcing, to help care for a relative's child, to be closer to school, or for any number of other reasons. One of the consequences of this migration for our study was the loss of subjects toward the end of it. A strike by schoolteachers closed the school, and close to 25 percent of those we had first weighed and measured in March were not in the village when we went to remeasure in November. Of the 106 youths studied, only 43 (41 percent) reside in the same household with their parents. The

TABLE 3.1
Marriages in Ebiama

	MALES	FEMALES
Presently married	60	112
Widowed or divorced	1	11
Bachelor	1	
Unknown	1	1
Total	63	123

	NUMBER OF WIVES OR HUSBANDS				TOTAL
	1	2	3	4 OR MORE	
Males					
Presently married	26	21	9	4	60
	(43%)	(35%)	(15%)	(10%)	(100%)
Total marriages	17	17	12	16	61
	(28%)	(28%)	(20%)	(26%)	(100%)
Females					
Presently married	112				112
	(100%)				(100%)
Total marriages	84	27	9	2	122
	(69%)	(22%)	(7%)	(2%)	(100%)

NOTE: Percentages are rounded to the nearest whole number and therefore add up to more than 100 percent.

remainder are related to the heads of households as follows: 34 (32 percent) are related through their mothers or sisters; 21 (20 percent) through their fathers or brothers; 4 (4 percent) live with their husbands; and the family relationship of 3 (3 percent) cannot be ascertained. Only one girl, from another Ijo village, lives with a family to which she is not related; she shares membership in the same Christian sect with them.

The total population of the PSU is 598, including 23 individuals who are unrelated to heads of households; 3 students from nearby villages, which do not have advanced classes; 8 policemen and their families; and 2 men working on construction projects, and their families. The indigenous Ijo population, totaling 575, resides in 68 households, 58 headed by men, 10 by women. Of the total of 253 men, 61 are or were married; only one man of marriageable age has remained a bachelor. Of 322 women, 123 are or were married. No adult women have remained unmarried. Although 43 percent of the

TABLE 3.2
The PSU in Ebiama

AGE	SIBA-OSIGIRI			GENERAL SAMPLE		
	M	F	TOTAL	M	F	TOTAL
0–4	46	49	95			
5–9	42	38	80			
10–14	42	51	93	26	30	56
15–19	39	35	74	21	24	45
20–24	13	14	27	1	4	5
25–29	9	14	23			
30–39	14	25	39			
40–49	11	9	20			
50–59	16	11	27			
60–69	4	7	11			
70–	4	10	14			
Unknown	13	59	72			
Total	253	322	575	48	58	106

men are presently married to one wife, 72 percent have been married more than once. Only 31 percent of the women have had more than one husband. The number and plurality of marriages are summarized in table 3.1.

Youths in our general sample are found in 35 of the former households and 4 of the latter. As described in the previous chapter, household membership is mobile and variable. During our census, households ranged in size from 1 to 28 individuals. Those households in which members of the general sample reside average 12 for male-headed households and 6 for female-headed ones.

Tables 3.2 and 3.3 summarize the age distribution of the PSU and of the youths selected for our samples.

Of the 16 males interviewed and observed in the intensive sample, 3 were identified as in the pre-growth-spurt stage, 12 as in the growth spurt stage, and 1 in the post-growth-spurt stage. Of the 10 females, the comparable numbers were 4, 2, and 4.

To illustrate the breadth of differences in household compositions, the following examples are drawn from Ebiama.

The Ebiki and Sogio Households

Jack Ebiki, who estimates that he was born in 1930, has twenty-five individuals living in his household, including three small-dowry

TABLE 3.3
Characteristics of the Samples in Ebiama

	GENERAL SAMPLE			LONG INTERVIEW			INTENSIVE SAMPLE		
AGE	M	F	TOTAL	M	F	TOTAL	M	F	TOTAL
10	2	4	6	0	1	1			
11	4	3	7	1	0	1	1	0	1
12	3	5	8	1	2	3	1	2	3
13	8	10	17	4	3	7	3	3	6
14	9	8	17	6	2	8	5	1	6
15	3	8	12	1	4	5	0	3	3
16	7	8	15	5	4	9	4	1	5
17	1	3	4						
18	5	1	6	2	0	2	2	0	2
19	5	4	9	2	1	3			
20	0	4	4						
24	1	0	1						
Total	48	58	106	22	17	39	16	10	26

wives and a big-dowry wife inherited from his father. The children range in age from newly born to nineteen years of age. Thomas Sogio, born approximately in 1947, has one wife, Yali. Three of their children and one other child related to Yali reside with them. The children's ages range from seven to sixteen.

The Ebiki household occupies three dwellings, which open toward each other around a courtyard, as depicted in map 3.1. A fourth building contains four rooms, three of which are kitchens used by two of Jack's wives, Porona (room no.13) and Meun (no.14), and a neighbor (no.12). The big-dowry wife, Desu, occupies the last room (no.15), using it to cook and sleep in. Maryann, Jack's other wife, has her kitchen in one of the rooms (no. 4) of the largest house in the compound. Here too are the bedrooms for each of the three wives, and one for Jack (no.1). Jack's room is the only one that does not have its own entrance from the verandah; a "sitting room" (no.2) where guests are received is the entry to his room (see table 3.4).

Maryann, Jack's first wife, has no idea how old she is, but we estimate she is forty-two years old, ten years younger than Jack. She has borne ten children; three died in infancy. Six children sleep with her in her bedroom (no.3). Jack's second wife, Porona, is estimated to be thirty-four years old. Four of her children have survived; five died at birth or during early infancy. Meun, approximately thirty-seven years old, the last wife, divorced her previous husband with whom

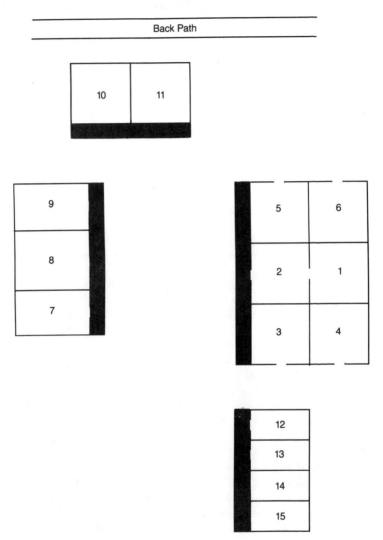

Map 3.1 The Ebiki compound

she had six children; three died at birth. The others are grown and live in other towns. With Jack she has had five children, three of whom died within a year of birth. Only her daughter, Diane, age ten, who is in standard 3, sleeps in her bedroom (no.6). Her other child is

TABLE 3.4
Ebiki Compound Residents

NAME	AGE	SEX	RELATIONSHIP	ROOM NO.	CLASS
Jack Ebiki	52	M		1	
Maryann	42	F	wife	3	
Bulaghe	16	M	son	7	standard 7
Ekpebarere	13	F	daughter	3	standard 4
Elisabeth	11	F	daughter	3	standard 3
Samuel	8	M	son	3	primary 2
William	6	M	son	3	primary 2
Dalles	13	F	Jack's father's sister's son's daughter	3	standard 4
Porona	34	F	wife	13	
Alaka	13	M	son	8	standard 6
Enwenowei	9	M	son	13	primary 2
Agirigeri	6	F	daughter	13	primary 1
Tomini	1	M	son	13	
Elepeinese	13	F	Porona's mother's mother's sister's daughter's daughter	13	
Meun	37	F	wife	14	
Christmas	12	M	son	8	standard 4
Diane	10	F	daughter	14	standard 3
Desu		F	wife	15	
Bolo		F	Jack's father's brother's daughter	10	
Betty	19	F	Bolo's daughter	9	
Teke	12	M	Bolo's son	10	
Dima	6	M	Bolo's son	10	
Sonora	15	F	Bolo's sister's daughter	9	

a boy, Christmas, who sleeps in the building across the courtyard from the main house.

There are two rooms in the last building. One (no. 10) is occupied by Bolo, Jack's father's brother's daughter, and two of her sons, Teke and Dima, twelve and six years old, respectively. Bolo divorced the father of her three children and is residing in Jack's compound until she moves to her new husband's quarter. Two boys from another village sleep in the other room (no. 11). Their father is related distantly to Jack's mother. They are here to attend school and both are in standard 8.

Thomas's compound is one building and a small kitchen (see map 3.2). The layout of his house is similar to Jack's: his room (no. 2)

Back Path

Kitchen

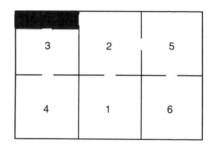

3	2	5
4	1	6

Map 3.2 The Sogio compound

is entered from a sitting room (no.1) that opens onto a verandah. The other rooms are occupied as follows:

His wife, Yali, sleeps with Reason, her mother's brother's daughter, who is sixteen years old, in room number 3. Yali and Thomas have had five children, two of whom died. The three sleep in another room. During the course of the year, several others resided here. Thomas's mother's sister's daughter and her two young children slept in a room (no.4) next to Yali's for a few months before leaving town to join her husband. Yali's younger brother, Albert, thirteen years old, also slept in the house (room no.6) for several months until he returned to his own parents' house in another quarter (see table 3.5).

The variations between the two households in size and in the kinds of relationships found in each are typical; it is also typical to find the membership of the household changing throughout the year. What is atypical are the particular features of each household. The monogamous marriage in the case of Thomas and Yali, and their intention to maintain it, is uncommon. The opposite dimension, which is somewhat less unusual, is Jack's large polygynous family.

Being a teacher is not an atypical occupation; both Yali and Thomas teach, and both Thomas and Jack teach elsewhere. Jack teaches in Oporoma, an hour's trip by motor launch from Ebiama. The close proximity and the school vacations or teachers' strikes meant that Jack frequently was at home. Thomas was fulfilling his youth corps commitment, required after completing the teacher's

TABLE 3.5
Sogio Compound Residents

NAME	AGE	SEX	RELATIONSHIP	ROOM NO.	CLASS
Thomas Sogio	35			2	
Yali	32	F	wife	3	
Juaa	13	F	daughter	5	standard 4
Apiapia	11	M	son	5	primary 2
Trust	7	M	son	5	
Reason	16	F	Yali's mother's brother's daughter	3	

training college, by teaching in the northern part of Nigeria. His visits during the year were infrequent.

The presence of absence of the head of the household has little effect on the activities of the household. Youngsters may be on call more frequently to deliver messages or perform small tasks for their fathers, but otherwise their daily routines tend to center around their mothers.

Yali completed her standard 6 class and then attended a teacher's training college for five years at a town on the coastal fringe of the delta. She returned to Ebiama and married Thomas the next year. She teaches primary 2, the class her son happens to be in. Apart from teaching, her daily schedule is not too different from Jack's wives, who are farmers or work on the oil palm plantation. They prepare meals in the morning before departing for work and then return in the afternoon to cook the evening meal. Yali must tend her farms on weekends, and obviously cannot depend on them for food as much as the other women do for their households' consumption. Nevertheless, being a teacher earns one a salary, and money is as essential as farm crops for sustaining a household because fish must be purchased for the most part. For this reason Meun, for example, who farms regularly, still prefers to work on the plantation when employment there is available.

THE PSU IN AMAKIRI

As previously mentioned, the quarters in Amakiri are, in geneological terms, patrilineal descent groups and exogamous for the most part; spatially, they are segments of Torowei clan. We selected two of Amakiri's seven named quarters, Makido I and Makido II, on the basis of the PSU criteria we described. In addition to being a self-identified interactive unit with temporal and spatial stability, the quarters also met the additional requirement of containing a sufficient number of youngsters of both sexes.

Makido quarters are located in the center of Amakiri. They contain a number of small shops, a guesthouse, one of the two revivalist churches, and a number of shrines, but neither the main market, nor the schools, nor any of the major churches or business establishments are within their limits. Thus, they are primarily residential quarters, which are exceptional only by the fact that both of Amakiri's elected representatives to the Bendel State House of Assembly reside in Makido I.

The Makido quarters were one quarter until 1920, when they subdivided because of disputes—referred to as a "civil war"—over building plots. Lineage members trace their descent from a common ancestor and therefore consider themselves to be all related to each other. They are grouped, however, into about six large families or family groups which usually bear one surname.

Our census of the two quarters in mid-1982, summarized in tables 3.6 and 3.7, counted a total of 989 persons; 467 males and 522 females. The age distribution indicates a high fertility rate and a relatively short life expectancy. In the Makidos, as in the populations of most developing countries, the proportion of population under age ten is high: 59 percent (236) of the males and 40 percent (206) of the females. Slightly higher percentages pertain to the under-twenty age-group, 60 percent and 50 percent, respectively.

Of the 29 males interviewed and observed in the intensive sample, 6 were identified as in the pre-growth-spurt stage, 15 as in the growth spurt stage, and 6 in the post-growth-spurt stage. Of the 30 females, the comparable numbers were 2, 17, and 11.

Like the rest of Amakiri, the Makidos also contain migrants, either in-marrying females or entire families, mostly Isokos and Urhobos, who have come to trade or set up businesses. Of the total PSU population, 410 are migrants, of whom more than 25 percent (115) are women married to Amakiri natives and for all intents and purposes are assimilated into the community. Only one male migrant is married to a native Amakiri woman. The remaining number includes 165 males, of whom 80 are adults, and 130 females, of whom 45 are adults. In contrast to the women, who usually take up permanent

TABLE 3.6
The PSU in Amakiri

AGE	MAKIDO I&II			GENERAL SAMPLE		
	M	F	TOTAL	M	F	TOTAL
0–4	80	60	140			
5–9	86	74	160	2	5	7
10–14	70	72	142	38	31	69
15–19	50	47	97	19	25	44
20–24	39	41	80			
25–29	21	34	55			
30–39	32	51	83			
40–49	36	51	87			
50–59	25	35	60			
60–69	23	33	56			
70–	5	26	31			
Total	467	524	991	59	61	120

residence, men return to their hometowns when they are ready to retire.

Makido natives, on the other hand, exhibit a high rate of out-migration. Past age twenty-five, only a handful of males and a small number of females remain in the community. In the age-group between thirty-five and forty-five, none of the older siblings of the youth in our sample is resident in the community, and only a few mem-

TABLE 3.7
Characteristics of the Samples in Amakiri

AGE	GENERAL SAMPLE			LONG INTERVIEW			INTENSIVE SAMPLE		
	M	F	TOTAL	M	F	TOTAL	M	F	TOTAL
8	0	2	2						
9	2	3	5						
10	4	2	6						
11	6	2	8						
12	12	8	20	6	5	11	4	3	7
13	11	11	22	8	8	16	4	3	7
14	5	8	13	4	3	7	3	3	6
15	8	9	17	4	6	10	3	5	8
16	3	6	9	3	3	6	2	2	4
17	2	5	7	2	2	4	2	2	4
18	1	3	4	1	0	1	1	0	1
19	5	2	7						
Total	59	61	120	29	30	59	19	18	37

bers of each sex are present between the ages of twenty-five and thirty-five. These individuals are not necessarily lost to the community, however. By age forty-five, there is a gradual increase in the number of native males as they return after a period of employment elsewhere.

Makido quarters contain 131 households of varying sizes. Individuals in our sample resided in 71 of these. Most families live in multiple-unit buildings or compounds, and two out of three of the youth in our sample reside in this kind of living arrangement. The remainder (21 of 71) reside in nuclear family households and single dwellings.

Patrilocal, virilocal residence is most usual. Eighty-one households are in the husband's father's quarter, and almost all of them are adjacent to the husband's father's compound. Nineteen households are located in the wife's father's quarter, 14 of which are in his own compound. Thirty-one families rent houses in the Makidos; they are Isokos and Urhobos who have no relatives there. Forty-six of Makidos' families are polygynous, 21 are monogamous, and 37 are headed by women, either divorced, separated, or widowed. Four of these women have husbands who reside elsewhere and occasionally visit. There are ten families in which the marital situation is unclear. The rest of the households consist of single transient renters.

The number of wives in the polygynous unions ranges from two to six. There is only one example of the latter in Amakiri, and two wives are by far the most usual number. Of the 160 women on whom reliable data are available (mothers and grandmothers of the adolescents), 116 have been at one time or are presently in polygynous unions. Of these same 160 women, 38 have been married more than once. The majority of the fathers have been at one time or are currently married in polygynous unions, although some of the wives may not reside locally. As far as could be determined, only 20 out of the total of 103 adult men living in the PSU have never been polygynously married. Three of these are Ijos; the rest of them are Isokos or Urhobos.

While the core group of individuals in the households most frequently consists of the male household head, his wife or wives, and their children, this is by no means always true. Most core groups contain a number of people who are related to either the husband or the wife, but most frequently to the former. Usually these individuals are the children of the husband or the wife from former unions. A large number of houses also contain children of the siblings of either husband or wife, and many of them have resident children of more or less distant relatives who are schooling in Amakiri. Grandchildren (children of either son or daughter) are also frequently present. Some households contain grandparents, a child's mother's mother, as well as his or her father's mother. Other frequent occupants include the unmarried brothers or sisters of the household head or of his wife. In all, there are thirty-seven categories of relatives who live in various households besides the core relationships of husband-wife, parent-child, and sibling-sibling.

Our subjects therefore live with individuals of a variety of ages who are related to them by different ties. Nevertheless, the typical residence for a youth is in the father's compound. Of our 120 youth, 83 (69 percent) live in the compound owned by his or her father. Of this number, 63 had both father and mother present, but in 20 cases the mother was absent due to divorce or separation. Two reside with the father's father. The remaining 30 live with a variety of relatives, the most frequent (12) of which was with the mother. All these mothers are Makido natives who returned to their own paternal compounds after divorcing their husbands. Other residences included that of the mother's brother (1), of the father's sister (6), of the mother's sister (2), and of distant patrilineal relatives (2). Several young males rented rooms in the quarter and had no relatives in the town.

The size of households varies. Larger ones may have twenty to thirty occupants, but the constituent household units of women and their children range from three to ten. These are the living domains in which the everyday lives of individuals unfold. It is with this group that children work, eat, and sleep and where their primary responsibilities lie. Children who do not have their mother present are usually cared for by another wife of the father, the grandmother, or an aunt.

As indicated in the previous chapter, eating and sleeping are usually done in these groups, the focus of which is the mother or a mother-surrogate. A mother and her prepubertal children are assigned one room in which they all sleep, many of them sharing beds or mats. Older children sleep with siblings or age-mates of their own sex in separate rooms. If no rooms are available in the father's compound, they frequently sleep in a neighboring compound with a child of similar age.

The majority of our subjects share a room with several individuals. Only fifteen had their own rooms, eleven of them boys and four girls, all of whom were over sixteen years of age. Twenty-two pre- and postpubertal girls and prepubertal boys shared a room with the mother. No boy over sixteen shared a room with his mother. Rooms are most frequently shared by combinations of siblings of both sexes at different ages, with the exception of girls sharing a room with an older brother. None of our females, whose ages ranged from nine to twenty, shared a room with a brother who was older than she. No subject shared a room with a father or with a grandfather, unless the mother was also present. In five monogamous families, the entire family, including mother and father and all children, slept in one room. Apart from the immediate family, other roommates for the youngsters included grandmothers, other adult females such as the father's sister or father's other wife, and age-mates who were both relatives and nonrelatives.

Sharing beds was most common among siblings of the same sex. Only four girls shared a bed with a brother, who were all toddlers. Three boys shared beds with a sister. The ages of the boys ranged from eight to thirteen years. The majority of the older subjects of both sexes (twenty-seven) had their own beds. Three of the oldest boys and six of the oldest girls, however, shared with unrelated age-mates. None of the boys or girls in the PSU shared a bed with either the mother or the father. One girl shared with a grandmother and one with a father's sister.

To describe these sleeping arrangements as we have done, and in the way our informants, old and young, reply to our questions, misses a typical feature of Ijo household compositions, mentioned several times already: its flux. The place where one actually spends the night is not always the same. Many of our subjects had more than one place to sleep and shifted around from father's to age-mates' to grandmothers' compounds. What is constant, however, is that wherever they sleep, they sleep with others and not alone. As they get older, their bedmates are increasingly limited to individuals of their own age and sex.

The differences in household composition are illustrated by the description of the following two households, the Ekberi and the Odozi.

Our first example from Amakiri is the Ekberi compound, outlined in map 3.3, which consists of a rectangle of low mud-brick buildings around a central courtyard. This is the home of Timinepere, an adolescent girl who serves in subsequent chapters to illustrate the

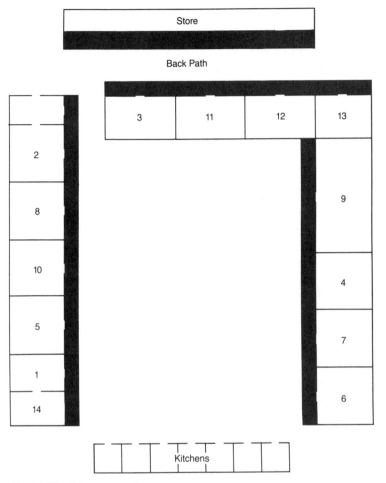

Map 3.3 The Ekberi compound

activities and behaviors of our youngsters. Igbideh Ekberi, seventy years old, is the head of the Ekberi compound. His half brothers Eneyi and Blessing also live here with their wives and children. Igbideh is an herbalist and a masseur and also runs a store across the road from his compound. This is where he spends most of his time and where he also sleeps. Igbideh is the oldest living male member of his sublineage and as such represents the highest authority for all members of this descent group. Eneyi and Blessing are five and ten years younger than Igbideh, respectively. Eneyi's occupations include trading and hauling gravel for construction companies with his boat. Blessing is also a trader and a tailor. Like Igbideh, he also has a small store fronting the main road where he sleeps. Eneyi has no store; he spends his nights in a room adjacent to those of his wives.

Igbideh has two wives in his household, Tubolayefa and Okubere with six and five children respectively. Tubolayefa is forty-two and has six children, three boys and three girls: Obukwohwo, twenty (male); Timinepere, fourteen (female); Ebimieowei, ten (male); Tarere, seven (female); Kemepuado, five (male); and Jenny, two (female). Tubolayefa had two miscarriages after Jenny was born and is pregnant once again. Although she has already had four sons with Igbideh, she wants to continue having children as long as she is able in order to maintain the favor of her husband. Okubere, her youngest co-wife, is only thirty years old and already has five children (see table 3.8).

Tubolayefa is primarily a farmer. She also does some fishing and petty trading, mostly selling her farm produce and fish at the Amakiri market and on the road fronting the Ekberi compound. With five children in school, her life is a constant struggle to make ends meet. It is her income that provides for the daily needs of her children and for their clothing. Igbideh helps with the books and school uniforms. As soon as her children are physically able, they help her on the farm, around the house, and in trading.

Tubolayefa and her children have one room, next to those of Ekberi's other wives, in a building that has a long, covered porch (see map 3.3). Each room has its own entrance to the porch. Their room has two beds; one is shared by two girls, Timinepere and Tarere, and the other by their mother and Jenny. Timinepere is fourteen years old, and we shall return to a description of her activities. Her two younger brothers sleep on a mat on the floor. Obukwohwo moved out of this room when he was sixteen and now shares a room with half brothers of similar age across the compound. During the day Tubolayefa and her children work at various tasks and eat on the porch area in the front of their room. Tubolayefa also has her own kitchen where she keeps her dishes and cooks on a woodburning stove.

The older children attend school, but they must still assume their share of the household and farm chores. Timinepere's responsibilities include sweeping her mother's part of the compound, washing dishes, gathering firewood for cooking, fetching water from the tap, washing her own school uniform, watching and bathing Jenny, ac-

TABLE 3.8
Ekberi Compound Residents

NAME	AGE	SEX	RELATIONSHIP	ROOM NO.	CLASS
Igbideh		M		1	
Tubolayefa		F	wife no. 1	4	
Obukwohwo	20	M	so	5	standard 2
Timinepere	14	F	da	4	primary 4
Ebimieowei	10	M	so	4	primary 2
Tarere	7	F	da	4	
Kemepuado	5	M	so	4	
Jenny	2	F	da	4	
Okubere		F	wife no. 2	6	
5 children	mo. to 10 yrs			6	
(Akpoebi)		F	wife no. 3		
Joseph	26	M	so	5	
Akboerere	20	F	da	7	
(3 children)					
(Egberighaere)		F	wife no. 4		
Matthew	16	M	so	5	standard 4
(Nisome)		F	wife no. 5		
Blessing		M		2	
(Penaere)		F	wife no. 1		
Oyinkoro	17	M	so	5	standard 5
(5 children)	5–14 yrs				
Mandi		F	wife no. 2	8	
Regina	16	F	da	8	standard 4
(Grace)	20	F	da		
(Victoria)	24	F	da		
Selena		F	wife no. 3	9	
4 children	6–14 yrs				
Lucy		F	wife no. 4	10	
2 daughters				10	
(2 sons)					
4 children	7 mos.–7 yrs			10	
(Wife no. 5)					
(3 children	2–7 yrs)				
(Wife no. 6)					
(2 children	mos.–3 yrs)				
Eneyi		M		3	
Enikeyen		F	wife no. 1	11	
Ajikwe	15	M	so	5	standard 3
Christopher	12	M	so	11	primary 5
Oyibonano		F	wife no. 2	12	
(5 children)					
(Ayama)		F	wife no. 3		
Ebiakpo	14	M	so	13	standard 2
Premobowei	12	M	so	13	standard 1

NOTE: Parentheses ( ) indicate residence elsewhere.

companying her mother to the farm for entire days, and occasionally selling fish. She is constantly at the beck and call of her father and his brothers, who send her on errands all around the town. Her leisure time is limited to a few opportune moments in the afternoon when she sneaks out to play on the street with her age-mates. She usually does her homework in the evenings when she shares a kerosene lantern with her brothers.

Okubere's children's ages range from newlyborn to ten years old. Igbideh has children by three other women from whom he is now divorced. His senior wife, Akpoebi, left him after she reached menopause and moved back to her father's compound in another quarter in Amakiri. She and Igbideh had five children of whom two, Joseph, twenty-six, and Akboerere, twenty (female), still live with their father. Akboerere attends secondary school; Joseph is considered mentally ill and has no work. Two other daughters are married and live elsewhere. Igbideh sent another wife, Egberighaere, back to her hometown across the river after the birth of a boy because he found her too quarrelsome. Their son, Matthew, is sixteen years old and has been living with Igbideh since he was four. He was looked after by Akpoebi first and now by Tubolayefa. His mother is remarried and has not seen him for years. He attends secondary school, where his expenses are paid by Igbideh.

His third ex-wife, Nisome, left Igbideh and went home to Aruware, her natal quarter in Amakiri, with her three children who are now between sixteen and twelve years of age. She refused to send the children back to their father, and Igbideh did not pursue the matter. Their relationship was so bitter he did not want her children, he told us.

The wives of all three brothers live in similar arrangements—each sharing a room with their prepubescent children. The older children sleep with cousins or siblings of their own sex in separate rooms. Igbideh's household resides in the building bordering the left-hand side of the compound, with Blessing's on the right and Eneyi's facing the road. The kitchens are in the back, as are some small structures used for taking baths. The large central area is common ground. This is where the children play and where the ancestors are buried. Unlike a number of similar compounds, the Ekberi compound has no shrines since they are Christians. A special parlor in Igbideh's part of the buildings is used for receiving guests and for holding meetings. This is considered private space, reserved primarily for the men. Women and children enter only by invitation.

Eneyi has two of his wives living with him. When he married the senior one, Enikeyen, she was a widow with four children. Of them, only fifteen-year-old Ajikwe stays with her mother; two other daughters are married elsewhere, and a son remained in his father's compound. Enikeyen and Eneyi have one son, twelve-year-old Christopher. With his second wife, Oyibonano, he has five children, all of whom are grown and live elsewhere. Eneyi is still married to a third woman, Ayama, but she recently went to stay with her father and a divorce may follow. Her two sons, Ebiakpo, fourteen, and Premoboere, twelve, are with Eneyi. They cook and take care of themselves without assistance, receiving money for food from Eneyi, who bitterly complains, saying their mother should be responsible for feeding them.

Blessing has six wives, three of whom live in the compound. The senior, Penaere, lives in her father's compound since her bride-price has not been paid. This did not prevent her, however, from bearing six children for Blessing. Her firstborn, Oyinkoro, seventeen, is Blessing's senior son and as such has special privileges. While most of the time Oyinkoro eats with his mother, he sleeps and spends most of his time in the Ekberi compound with his half brothers and cousins.

Two other wives live in rooms rented for them by Blessing in nearby buildings due to lack of space in the compound. They have three and two children, respectively, ranging from one to twelve years of age. The children usually spend their days in the Ekberi compound with the other children. The first resident's wife, Mandi, has been married to Blessing since 1958 but has only borne three daughters, which somewhat diminishes her status, even though she is the senior wife living with him. Only one of these girls still resides there, sixteen-year-old Regina. Grace is a schoolteacher in a nearby community, and Victoria is married to a businessman in Warri.

Blessing inherited his second wife, Selena, from his brother after he died. At that time she had one child, a daughter, who is now a schoolteacher and lives in Warri. Selena and Blessing had four children subsequently, two of whom are in primary and two in secondary school.

Lucy, the third resident wife, was divorced from her first husband with whom she had five children. Of these, two girls aged eighteen and eleven and one son aged sixteen live with the mother; the other two sons remain with their father. After her marriage to Blessing, Lucy gave birth to four more children whose ages range from seven years to seven months. Blessing helps Lucy with expenses of his own children but not with those from her first marriage. These are assisted by their father's family and by Lucy's mother who lives at the other end of Makido. All the wives of the Ekberi brothers are farmers and traders. With the exception of Lucy, none of them has had more than one or two years of schooling. All of the present generation of children attend school.

This crowded, noisy compound, with wives cooking, pounding and selling, older children busily scurrying around, and small children playing in the courtyard, is the center of Timinepere's world. She is proud to be part of a large compound and to have a father who has many children and many wives. Although the Ekberis are not considered a wealthy family, they are one of the most respected ones in the quarter, largely due to their size.

Timinepere's life at age fourteen is very similar to that of other girls her age. Prepubescent girls are expected to carry quite a bit of responsibility and to perform the kinds of chores previously described. One major difference between her experience and that of others is that while she is kept busy around the house and on her mother's farm, she is not expected to work after school in a store or to hawk bread or cold drinks at the market. As a consequence, Timinepere has been able to attend school regularly and to pay attention to her studies. She is in form 2 of secondary school, where she should be for her age. Most other girls have had to repeat classes in primary school, since they were kept too busy to attend regularly.

Girls who are older by some years, starting around age fifteen or sixteen, become full-fledged helpmates of their mothers. Women who have daughters around this age can devote full time to farming, fishing, and trading, knowing that the daughters are in charge. These girls take over the running of the household unit, directing the sibling work force, cooking, grinding, doing all the laundry, and raising the small children. Between their early morning and afternoon chores, most of them attend secondary school, returning home around one o'clock, when they switch roles from schoolgirl to housekeeper.

The second illustration is the Odozi household, outlined in map 3.4; it is the home of Omiebi Odozi, a fourteen-year-old boy who is the eldest son of Benson Odozi, who divorced Omiebi's mother when he was a baby. His mother returned to her hometown but sent Omiebi back to the father when Omiebi was two years old. By then Ben-

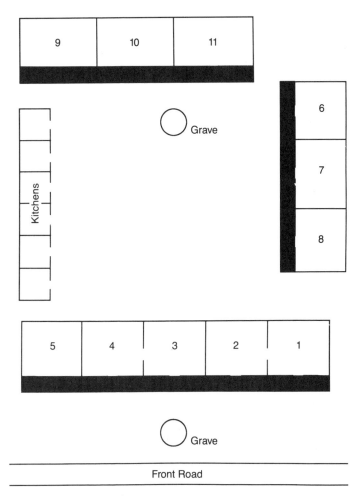

Map 3.4 The Odozi compound

son was married to Christiana, his current wife, who gave birth to a daughter, Hope, the year Omiebi came to live with them. At that time Benson had another wife with whom he had two daughters, Evelyn, now fifteen, and Yintare, now twelve. This marriage did not work out either, and the mother of the girls left Amakiri, leaving the children with Benson and Christiana. Christiana subsequently gave birth to

TABLE 3.9

Odozi Compound Residents

NAME	AGE	SEX	RELATIONSHIP	ROOM NO.	CLASS
F. O. Odozi		M		6	
Nanu		F	wife no. 1	7	
Edit		F	wife no. 2	8	
Oya		F	deceased bro no. 1's wife	9	
Benaebi		F	deceased bro no. 1's wife's da	10 and 11	
Benaebi's 2 sons and their wives				10 and 11	
Benson		M	deceased bro no. 2's wife no. 1's so	1	
(Wife no. 1) Omiebi	14	M	so	2	standard 2
(Wife no. 2) Evelyn	15	F	da	1	standard 3
Yintare	12	F	da	1	standard 1
Christiana		F	wife no. 3	1	
Hope	12	F	da	1	primary 6
Oyiadeyinfa	9	M	so	2	primary 2
Etemoere	5	F	da	1	
Tokere	3	M	so	1	
Lydia		F	deceased bro no. 2's wife no. 2	5	
Sunday		M	browiso	3	
(Binaebi)		F	wife no. 1	3	
Harriet	18	F	da	4	standard 5
Victor	14	M	so	4	standard 3
Helen		F	wife no. 2	3	
Ebiere	10	M	so	3	primary 3
Tare	7	M	so	3	primary 2
Elaye	6	F	da	3	primary 1

two sons, Oyindeyinfa, nine, and Tokere, three, and to a daughter, Etemoere, five. She is now Benson's only wife and as such takes care of a total of seven of his children from various unions. Neither she nor Benson desire any more children, and Benson claims that he wants to remain monogamous (see table 3.9).

Christiana is a farmer, trader, and seamstress. She has a foot-pedaled sewing machine on her front porch where she works long hours during the day. From this vantage point she can direct the work of her children, Evelyn, Omiebi, Yintare and Hope, who are all responsible for sweeping, fetching, carrying, washing, and infant care. Because Christiana is Benson's only wife, they share the responsibility of feeding and clothing the children. Benson is a teacher at the primary school in Amakiri and as such is assured a steady and predictable cash income. With the additional money that Christiana earns, they are one of the more affluent local families. This, however, does not diminish the amount of work that an Amakiri mother of seven has to accomplish, and the help of the children is no less important than in other families.

Benson, his wife, and children sleep in a two-room unit which is at one end of a long building shared with Benson's half brother, Sunday, and Sunday's mother. It was built by their father shortly before he died, and he is buried in the courtyard in front of it. His grave is marked by a group of small bushes. The sons say they plan to install a permanent grave marker, perhaps one made of marble. Their father was not a Christian, whereas some of the brothers are, and this causes some disagreements among them regarding the proper monument that should be erected.

One of Benson's rooms serves as a parlor during the day, and the couch in it is used as a bed at night. The parents share one bed, and most of the children double up on the couch or on sleeping mats. Sunday's family has the same amount of space, shared by him, his wife, Helen, their children—Ebiere, ten, Tare, seven, Elaye, six— and two of Sunday's children from other unions—Harriet, eighteen, and Victor, fourteen. Sunday's mother, Lydia, has one room. Each of the three women, Christiana, Helen and Lydia, has her own kitchen in a separate building at the far end of the compound.

Sunday is also a schoolteacher who currently attends the University of Ibadan where he is studying for a B.S. degree to qualify as secondary school principal. Helen recently completed her teacher's certificate and started to teach in the secondary school in Amakiri. She was thirty-seven years old when she returned to school, a dream she had nurtured since her first marriage. Because her first husband did not allow her to study beyond the secondary school certificate, she divorced him after bearing him a son. Soon after, she married Sunday, who was willing to send her to school. She now reciprocates, supporting the children while he is studying.

In the building directly behind Benson's lives the head of the sublineage, F. O. Odozi, one of the respected elders of Makido. F.O. is the only survivor of the three senior Odozi brothers and as such is at least nominally married to all their surviving wives, including Lydia. Two of these women reside with him; Lydia and another widow, Oya, chose not to. F.O.'s house is currently shared by his two wives, the son of one, his wife, and four school-age children. Being head of the family gives F.O. authority over the rest of the members and a major role in making important decisions that concern them all. In matters of daily living, however, he does not interfere, and the younger male household heads are free to run their own family units.

Oya lives nearby in a house built by her husband before his death. He is buried in front of it. She shares the building with two of her married sons and their wives and children and with a son of her deceased husband by another wife. There are eight preschool and school-age children in her building, their ages ranging from one to eight years of age. Her nineteen-year-old daughter, Benaebi, recently joined the household after becoming pregnant while attending teacher's training in a nearby town. She expects to remain after the child is born until her bridewealth is paid by her future husband.

The everyday life of Omiebi is centered around his own small family unit where his activities are directed by his stepmother. The rhythm of this unit, however, is very much in unison with that of other similar family units, mostly with that of Sunday. So Omiebi is surrounded by half brothers and half sisters and cousins of all ages. He does his daily chores with his sisters, but whenever possible he runs errands with his cousin, Victor. Both boys are in form 2 of the secondary school, where they usually walk together. Their fathers consider education to be of prime importance, especially for boys, and both of them are conscientious and good students.

At age fourteen Omiebi is no longer engaged in all phases of housework as he was when he was younger. This is usual for young boys, who start assisting their mothers when they reach seven or eight. As opposed to girls, however, who with age take on increasing amounts of responsibility, boys as they get older shed their obligations around the house. Adolescent boys who have reached thirteen or fourteen are only very rarely recruited for menial household tasks. They are either allowed to attend school full time or take on paying part-time jobs after school hours.

COMPARING THE TWO PSUs

The PSU in Amakiri is almost twice the size of the one in Ebiama —991 compared to 575. Even more contrastive, but consistent with the acculturative experience of each community, the Amakiri PSU contains 410 non-Ijo migrants, whereas the Ebiama PSU contains 23; by chance, in the latter case 23 is the total number of migrants in the whole village.

Despite the demographic and interethnic differences, the similarity between the households in each community is striking. Even though a far greater percentage (72 percent) of youth in Amakiri reside with both their parents than in Ebiama (41 percent), pervasive features of Ijo households in both places are their extensive range of relationships and their ever-changing composition. Paradoxically, we find a sense of permanency to the kinship network, rather than an insecurity about acceptance in the household. The extension of kinship ties through polygynous families and the reckoning of descent, whether patrilineally, matrilineally, or ambilineally, produce unquestioned attachments in time, no matter where the place.

■ 4
Life Stages

In the early or mid-teens a major physiological event, puberty, occurs in all normal humans. This physiological transition into reproductive maturity is marked by a sudden growth spurt in both males and females and by changes in body shape, in the proportion of muscle and fat, and in a number of physiological functions. Females experience the onset of menarche and the growth of breasts and pubic hair. In males, the growth of testes and penis, the appearance of pubic and facial hair, and a change in voice characterize this period of development. These changes are initiated in males by a large increase in the levels of testosterone and in females by the increase of estrogen levels in the blood. There is also evidence that, during the early phase of this growth period, the human brain undergoes significant physiological reorganization.

One of the persistent questions about this stage of life has been the relationship between physiological change and behavior. While physiological changes are universal, are there also universal correspondences in what is identified as "adolescent" behavior? We began with the assumption that adolescence, unlike puberty, is a culturally defined status that varies from society to society. Of course the meaning of puberty also varies with its cultural context and may indeed be affected by it, as illustrated by the significance of diet on the timing of the average menses. Nevertheless, puberty occurs whether or not a population treats it as a significant event; adolescence, on the other

64

hand, is more problematic, and the Ijo are an example of how a population can ignore it, at least until fairly recently.

The Ijo language specifies a number of life stages, none of which, however, corresponds directly to the English usage of the word *adolescence*. With the introduction of Western-style schooling and an expected delay in the age of marriage, the possibility of a prolonged period between puberty and marriage has come to define an adolescent period in the life stages of the present generation.

This chapter presents a brief set of data on the physiological changes that occur during puberty in the Niger Delta, reviews Ijo life stages, and indicates a new recognition of the adolescent period that has occurred in the Ijo conception of the life cycle. We also describe some of the difficulties we encountered in collecting the data.

PHYSIOLOGY

To determine the approximate period when puberty occurs we collected physiological data on height and weight. The subjects were weighed and measured a few months after the beginning and very near the end of the research periods. The first measurements were taken in Ebiama and Amakiri in March and April 1982, and the second in December 1982 and January 1983, respectively. Since a growth spurt is considered to be a more reliable indicator of puberty than weight gain, we relied on the rate of growth, along with our visual observations and knowledge of a female's menses, to assign individuals to a status of prepuberty, pubescent, or postpuberty. We determined the growth rates, or velocity, by multiplying the difference between the first and second measurements by the number of interval days, divided by 240. The latter number, the average number of days between measurements, was used to arrive at equivalent velocities for subjects who could not all be measured on the same day.

We encountered three major problems in obtaining physiological data. The first was the technical difficulty of recording height and weight accurately. Since we used ordinary bathscales and took height measurements by marking off walls with a tape measure, our data offer reliable measures of differences rather than valid numbers per se. The second was the mobility of our subject population. As mentioned earlier in our discussion of the PSUs, a goodly number of those initially present in the PSU were not there at the end. This was especially true of Ebiama, where a third of those weighed and measured at the beginning of our study were not present at the time of the second measurement.

Determining accurate chronological ages was the third and most time-consuming problem. Since only a few Ijo in Ebiama have recorded their birth dates, we had to use several techniques to arrive at an estimated birth date for each subject. These are described in chapter 3. Our confidence in the final age determinations of our general samples ranges from certainty to plus or minus a year.

Although we have data from only two Ijo communities, the differences in height between the two support an observation often heard that Ijo in the southern part of the Niger Delta tend to be shorter than those in the area nearest the mainland. In Amakiri the height for boys ranged between 127 cm and 175.5 cm; for girls the range was from 130 cm to 170.5 cm. In Ebiama the heights ranged from 126 cm to 172 cm, and from 118 cm to 168 cm, respectively. The maximum height velocity was reached at somewhat different times: for boys, in Amakiri the peak velocity of 3.08 was attained at age twelve; in Ebiama the peak of 3.97 was reached at age fourteen. For girls, in Amakiri the peak velocity of 3.57 occurred at age twelve, in Ebiama the comparable figures were 3.93 at age twelve.

In both communities the age of menarche was estimated to be between thirteen and fifteen years.

LIFE STAGES: PAST AND PRESENT

The Ijo recognize a number of named stages in the life cycle. These are not well-defined age-grades in the sense conceived of in many other African cultures, where cohorts have specific functions. Rather, the Ijo label individuals as being capable of performing certain tasks appropriate for them. Moving from one stage to another is dependent on physiological and mental development. Setting age limits for a period, as we do below, is somewhat arbitrary; chronological age was relevant in the past only in the important identification of relative age. "Birthdays" were unknown. The emphasis on comparative age continues in matters of social etiquette in that drinks, for example, should be passed to the eldest first, and in joking relations one is always a *kala tobou* ("small child") to an older person. The emergence of an

TABLE 4.1
Ijo Names for Age Periods

AGE PERIOD	MALE	EITHER SEX	FEMALE
Birth–2		ayapede	
2–5	kala tobou		kala eruoba
6–12			eruoba
6–14	kala awou		
13–19			ereso
15–25	kala pesi		
19–45			erera
25–45	asiai pesi		
45–60	okosi-otu palemo		okusi ere
60–		okosi-otu	

adolescent period in the life cycle, along with the status gained from schooling, gives absolute age more significance than in the past.

Table 4.1 is an approximate identification of age and age periods in Amakiri; the age periods have slightly different names in Ebiama but the dialectical variation does not represent major differences in expected behaviors.

The age labels in contemporary usage tend to use schooling as a criterion for defining the boundaries of an age period. *Kala tobou* now refers to preschool boys and those just beginning school and *kala eruoba* to girls of the same age. Then there are primary-school boys or girls, which *kala awo/eruoba* now implies. Secondary-school boys and girls are those called by *kala pesi/ereso,* respectively. The use of this institutional criterion has resulted in prolonging the period between childhood and adulthood and in fact has created a new substage for "older children still schooling," referred to as "big schoolgirls" or "big schoolboys," which we would define as a stage comparable to what is meant by "adolescence." In the past, this period was considered the appropriate time for girls to marry and for boys to participate in communal work.

Now, as before, children are very much desired by all adult Ijo. The birth of a child is greeted with happiness by males and females alike. Due to improving health and sanitary measures, infant and child mortality has declined in the past few decades, resulting in an increasing fertility rate for the community since most adult women still desire to become pregnant every two years. Parents in both communities claim to want several children of each sex, but in Amakiri they clearly prefer males and worry if only females are born. Males are important for the future of the patrilineage and for the past as well, since they must propitiate the dead elders. Men often explain that when their first wives were "too weak" to bear males and only gave birth to females, they were induced to seek second wives.

The youngest children (up to age two), referred to as *ayapede*, are considered helpless and in need of constant care and attention. A child in this category spends most of the time in close physical contact with the mother, being carried on her back to the farm or kitchen, or held on her lap while she performs other domestic tasks. At night the infant sleeps with the mother on her bed or sleeping mat. The child is breast fed on demand, and the breast is also used as a pacifier.

Few rituals mark the life cycle, but two occurred in the past within this period. One was held when the child's first tooth erupted. First the child was taken to one of the elders of the village to ensure that the tooth would not disappear. Then the head was shaved, and after three days for a male or four days for a female, the new hair was trimmed. The child's scalp was then decorated with white paint, cowry shells were placed around his or her waist, and the mother walked the child around the village.

The other ritual was a naming party, usually held at the time the first teeth appear, at which friends and relatives gathered to celebrate the occasion. This is done today, if at all, only for a woman's first child, and naming may be done at any time after birth. As in the past, anyone can suggest a name, and not infrequently a person may assume several names, both Ijo and English ones, during the course of childhood.

The native names are usually descriptive and refer to either a behavioral trait in the child or a circumstance surrounding its birth. The Ijo names often have no gender distinctions. Thus, a name such as *Emomotimi* (stay-with-me) may be used for a boy and a girl alike. English names, on the other hand are gender specific. During a lifetime, the individual may use either name, depending on the context. The majority of educated adults prefer to use their English names, but there is currently a growing tendency among young, educated Nigerians to use only native names.

Around two years of age the birth of a new sibling usually signifies the end of the close mother-child relationship. The *ayapede* (babies) become *kala tobou* (little, small, or young boys) or *kala eruoba* (little, small, or young girls) and are now completely weaned.

If they cry or protest, they are simply picked up by the mother and put outside the door. They are entrusted to the care and surveillance of older siblings who either carry them around or tag after them to make sure they do not fall into the river or into a cooking fire, but otherwise the youngsters are free to move around, explore, and play. Neighbors give them food from the cooking pots, and wherever the youngsters go people tease and play with them. They are not thought to be responsible for their actions and are only rarely chastised. When a child reaches about five years of age, especially if the child is the eldest of a mother, he or she is increasingly given simple chores to do. Discipline is still not strict and if the child is unwilling to work or obey, he or she is thought to be "stubborn" and may occasionally be yelled at but not often beaten. Little differentiation is made between boys and girls.

By six years of age, when children enter school and are responsible enough to take care of themselves, they enter the next age period. Girls are referred to as *eruoba* (girl), and boys as *kala awou* (young boy). A major change that has occurred in this generation is that both boys and girls are sent to school, whereas most of the mothers of the schoolchildren have had two or three years of schooling at most, and few of them are literate.

In many respects children are freer now than in the younger period. They no longer require constant supervision by an older sibling, and they are not yet required to participate fully in household tasks. Still, their labor is increasingly relied on in the household. They are given simple chores around the house and on the farm. They accompany the mother fishing and farming, and help in selling at the market or in the family's shop. They carry firewood, water, and supplies; they sweep, wash dishes and clothes, and begin to watch their younger siblings. Before the next age period, however, they will have learned to care for themselves and their wards, and to perform many of the tasks they will need to do as adults. In this stage, gender distinctions in the assignment of chores are not yet evident. Mothers will use whichever gender child is around in the appropriate age-group for these menial tasks. There are no recognized girls or boys chores, although if there are six-to-twelve-year-old children of either gender available, girls are more likely to be asked to tend a baby and boys to sweep. Similarly, in social behavior no distinctions are made between boys and girls in this age range. They are supposed to be responsible, respect their elders, and be available for service when called. Boys, however, seem to get away with more disobedience, and parents tolerate more "rascally" behavior from them even at this younger age. Responsibility and respectfulness are highly desired by parents of children in this age period, but discipline is not consistent. Disobedience may elicit punishment one day but not another. Children learn that hiding from the parent is often a successful technique for avoiding work and punishment.

Circumcision is prerequisite to male adulthood but it is not a marker of entry into a new life stage. Two generations ago boys were circumcised during this stage, at around seven or eight years of age. It was not an occasion marked by ritual, and it was done either individually or in groups of two or three. Now the operation is usually performed seven days after birth, and in Amakiri it is done by a doctor in the presence of the mother. As in the past, in Ebiama any man can perform the operation, but a few have gained a reputation for doing it.

As children become older, a definite gender distinction is made by their parents in their treatment. Beginning around twelve to fourteen years of age, boys are referred to as *kala pesi* (young person) until they have reached manhood at about the age of twenty-five. Girls are called *ereso* ("nubile" woman) until the age of nineteen. Boys are increasingly allowed to roam, to visit friends, and to play games. Appropriate social behavior for girls at this age increasingly involves staying around the house, not only because they are expected to work, but also because it is thought inappropriate for girls of this age to "stroll out." Boys of this age are usually found with large groups of same-gender friends, away from the house. Girls also have same-gender friends, but they visit each other in their homes and their group size tends to be much smaller.

Older boys are allowed to delegate most of their household chores to their younger brothers and sisters, but the girls become more and more burdened with work. Even though girls now also attend school full time, parents still expect them to perform all labor that was appropriate to females of their age level in their mothers' time. Although boys of fourteen are relatively free to roam and play after they return from school, girls immediately begin cooking or helping to sell fish or produce the mother has brought in during the day. By the time girls reach their midteens they are capable of running the household, permitting the mother to devote her entire time to trading or farming activities. Older boys are expected to prepare themselves for their future occupation, and in many cases this preparation is limited to studying for exams. Only a very few males in Amakiri, even in the preceding generation, learned their father's trade by accompanying him on hunting, fishing, or palm-berry-collecting trips. In Ebiama the change has been slower in that more males than in Amakiri learned the predominant occupations of the past, even though they may not practice them today. These striking differences in the behaviors of the genders, beginning at around age twelve, emerge from our spot observational data, which show that girls at this age and up worked at domestic chores three times as much as boys and spent half as much time in play. Members of this age-group are the main subjects of our study, and the remaining chapters describe this period of the life cycle.

Entry into adulthood varies considerably. In the past, one was either a child or an adult. The latter was determined by the attainment of the adult roles associated with marriage. For females, adulthood could arrive as soon as they were capable of bearing children, because at approximately the same time they had already learned the necessary skills for maintaining a household. Males married later because they required more time to acquire the physical maturity to perform their occupations and to earn sufficient money to support a household.

Traditionally, the stage of *kalapesi/ereso* was considered to be of "young adulthood." For boys, attainment of this stage of being "big enough" was signified by being required to participate in communal rituals and to supply the manpower at communal works. Males at this age, for example, are called on to dig a grave and females to cook for the visitors during a funeral. In Ebiama the ceremony performed when a boy successfully cut down his first bunch of palm fruit was a good indication that he had arrived at this stage. Although the stage did not take place in special schools or initiation camps, nor was entrance or exit from it marked by rituals, it was a period of training, learning, apprenticeship, and preparation for future roles and responsibilities. Boys would also be fully preoccupied in perfecting their skills of hunting, fishing, and palm oil producing, as well as making "gin" from palm wine and constructing houses.

For most women, entry into this stage of life coincided fairly closely with the onset of menarche and with marriage. The beginning of menstruation is not recognized with a ritual, but most girls used to be married either before or immediately after its onset.

Data on the mothers of the current generation of adolescents in

Amakiri indicate that the average age at marriage in the 1920s, 1930s, and 1940s was fifteen, approximately the same as the age for the onset of menses or slightly earlier. The average age at the birth of their first child was 16.5 in the 1920s and 17.5 in the 1930s and 1940s. To ensure an appropriate match, marriage was arranged by the parents or by senior members of the couple's lineages, often long before the girl reached puberty. Nevertheless, adults insist that a girl had to agree to the marriage or it could not be consumated.

In Ebiama, where age assessments are problematic for the reasons mentioned earlier, marriage and pregnancy histories are difficult to reconstruct. The practice in the past, as evidenced during our previous study in 1958, was for all females to be married by the time of or shortly after their menses, which we approximated as fourteen years of age. The average age at first birth of women born in the 1950s, for whom we have relatively precise data, was eighteen. The general opinion in Ebiama, as in Amakiri, is that girls cannot be forced to marry a man, regardless of their parents' wishes. Ijo claim that the objectives of arranging a marriage for a young girl were to strengthen the social relationships between the girl's father and her intended husband, or to help the father pay off a debt to another man. Of course, the profound value on having many children was the ostensible reason for marrying as young as possible.

Marriage is a long and elaborate process, whether it is big dowry or small dowry. Both procedures involve several steps over a period of time. Bridewealth includes cash payments to the bride and to her parents. The groom is also expected to give them numerous gifts and to donate his work as well. For example, in Amakiri the mother-in-law may receive a canoe and a yam barn as her share, and the father-in-law is entitled to help in building his new house.

Before a bride consents to have sexual relations with her husband, he also gives her special gifts, such as bedding, a mosquito net, and some cloths, as well as paying her a "sleeping fee." Frequently, a young wife remains with her parents, occasionally visiting her husband until she delivers a child. When she finally moves to his house, the husband gives a specified number of bottles of gin to his in-laws and is supposed to complete the payment of the bride-price. Her arrival at his house is celebrated by his kinsmen, who gather and drink to her health.

Even though a woman is adept at performing household tasks by the time of her marriage, when a young wife moves to her husband's house she is given instructions on how to cook and to farm by her mother-in-law or by an older co-wife. She may live with the older woman, cooking at her fire and helping her on the farm or with trading for a period of time lasting from a few months to a year. This period ends when the bride declares herself *ware anga* (capable of maintaining a household). If he has not already done so, her husband will give her cooking pots, an iron ring for holding a pot over the fire, and cooking utensils.

In Ebiama, five of twenty females between the ages of sixteen and twenty had married, and were not attending school, but one had not yet gone to reside with her husband. Of the remaining 15, 12 were in the primary or secondary school and 3 were not in school. The delayed marriage for a majority of those in the marriageable age range contrasts with the past, when all of them would have married. Only one of the females in our general sample became pregnant during the year. She was not one of the five who had married.

Girls of the present generation are postponing marriage because of schooling, but they are not delaying their sexual activity. Pregnancy is not an uncommon result. While they may produce babies, they are not marrying in the same sense as in the past. Pregnancy and schooling are not perceived as contradictory, although they are not necessarily a desired combination. No girl under twenty was married in the Amakiri PSU, whereas approximately half of the girls in the sample between the ages of sixteen and eighteen gave birth or became pregnant during the research period. In the case of the boys, they are not yet in a financial position to pay the marriage fees. Schoolgirls do not marry because their husbands would not allow them to continue in school, and because schooling may ultimately lead to employment as a teacher or in other, nonmanual jobs. Having a child is not interpreted as a contradiction to this attitude because in most extended households there are several available caretakers, and the girl may resume her schooling. Similarly, a woman is not prevented from taking a job as a result of having children.

Unmarried girls at this age are required to attend rituals and communal works like adults, since they are "big enough," but in Amakiri they are not allowed to attend the women's association meetings, which are limited to married women only. No similar disadvantage pertains to unmarried males, who are free to attend council meetings.

In this era of free primary education, most people consider that schoolchildren reach adulthood after they finish schooling, an event that usually occurs around eighteen to twenty years of age. The major concern of these young adults is making a decision about their future. Many of them want to continue their schooling and hope that either their father or another relative will pay their school fees. Others want to work and look around for employment either in the community or in nearby towns. The two or three years following graduation from secondary schools is a period of indecision for both males and females. The males take odd jobs, help out in the store, and leave for shorter or longer periods, only to return again. The females stay at home, taking care of their infants or helping their mothers. Some of them move in with the families of their boyfriends for a while, then go home again. Both sexes are involved in community work projects, attend ceremonies and family meetings as adults, and are treated as such to some extent. Most people recognize, however, that these young adults are in transition either to marriage, or to further schooling, or to a job in another town.

There is a striking contrast between what is required of a pregnant woman in Ebiama and Amakiri. In the latter, before a woman's first child is born, her clitoridectomy has to be performed. In Ebiama, individuals say they heard from elders that the operation was once performed in the village long ago, but no one in memory has done so. According to legend, seven girls died following the surgery, and this was interpreted as a sign from the water spirits that they did not want females to be circumcised.

In Amakiri the clitoridectomy is usually done in the seventh month of pregnancy. The husband (or if not yet married, the boyfriend) is responsible for paying a fee to the midwife, for buying a number of specified presents for his wife (or girlfriend), and for sponsoring a small celebration in her parents' home. If she has previously moved away, she now returns for the operation and for the delivery of her first child. Following the operation, the woman remains in the care of her mother, who dresses her wound with ointment and massages her body with camwood for a period of seven days. In recent times, the payments made during the marriage preliminaries are being replaced by the circumcision fees and gifts to the girl by the father of her child. Furthermore, more and more girls prefer to have their clitoridectomy done prior to becoming pregnant and either pay for the operation themselves or ask their fathers to pay for it. While it is possible to become circumcised without pregnancy, to deliver a child without the mother being circumcised is an abomination. An uncircumcised woman cannot be buried in the village because the fertility of the earth would diminish. If the operation is not performed, it is believed that the child will be devoid of human status and will bring harm to the village. Women circumcised during the year perform special dances during the town's annual spring festival, the *seigbein*, a twelve-day celebration of the ancestors and a purging of bad spirits from the town. Every woman has to perform the dance before she dies, whether she has had a child or not. If she dies without doing so, her daughter should dance in her place or the community's well-being would be endangered. A woman dances in the seigbein held in her natal quarter, and her expenses are born by her husband. The expenses include a number of special cloths she has to wear during the several days of the festival, coral beads, cowry shells, as well as drinks to her kinsmen and gifts of cash to her. Only non-Christians continue to perform the *ayo,* at the time of the next full moon after the seigbein is completed. This dance is believed to ensure their fertility, and they present gifts at the shrine located at the extreme southern end of the town.

Whereas in Ebiama the steady progression from childhood to womanhood is marked only by pregnancy, in Amakiri the recognized steps are of a different order. Pregnancy and clitoridectomy initiate womanhood; performing in the seigbein completes the process. There has been a growing tendency toward delaying the last step, however, because of the expenses associated with dancing in the seigbein. Consequently, virtually no young woman performs it after the birth of her first child. The most common age at which the ritual is now performed is between thirty and forty years of age. Nevertheless, a married woman, whether she has had children or whether she has performed the seigbein, may participate in the women's association in her husband's village.

No ceremonies marked the attainment of adulthood by the men at the age of around twenty-five. Their age reference, *asiai pesi* (mature person), no longer carried the connotation of "kala" (little, young, or small). Apart from having to shoulder increasing communal and family responsibilities, which come with their increasing age, there is less of a change in the lives of men at this stage than in the lives of women. Men begin to play an active role in community youth associations, which are important political action groups in both Ebiama and

Amakiri. Nevertheless, at this age very few men have the resources with which to build a house, so after marrying they continue to live in their father's compound, where a separate room is given to the new couple, or, more usually in modern times, they live away from the community and rent accommodations in a town. Women, on the other hand, are almost invariably married by the age of twenty-two. Referred to as *erera* (mature women), they have come to join their husbands and have to establish new sets of relationships.

Individuals in the next stage of adulthood (between forty-five and sixty years of age) are known as *okusi ere* (older women) and *okosi-otu palemo* (older men). This category is made up of mature adults who are responsible for the planning and organization of community projects and for the town's welfare. The town is administered by males, including the *amayanabo*, the headman of the town, and the court and quarter chiefs.

Women also have their own organization in Amakiri. A president is elected for the whole town. There are also a number of helpers from different quarters as well as a spokeswoman, a treasurer, a secretary, and a town crier for the whole town and one for each quarter. These women are responsible for organizing certain aspects of the seigbein, for settling disputes, and for discussing women's aspects of community development with the men. (The importance of these womens' associations was also noted by N. Leis, 1974.)

Individuals in this age period are key participants in leading various community ceremonies, but they are not exempt from communal labor projects. Most of the women are past childbearing age and have become grandmothers many times over. They occupy a central role in the lives of their children, especially in the help they provide as caretakers of grandchildren. Most men in this age-group have acquired second or third wives and continue to be both sexually and reproductively active. With the increase in the number of their descendants, they receive a great deal of respect. They have built their own houses and have become the major sources of opinion in the family councils.

The age of elder or *okosi-otu* is reached between sixty to seventy years of age. Men in this stage of life are often the mediators and the judicial officials of the community. In Amakiri, the oldest of them in each quarter are the caretakers of the sacred relics. Elders are exempt from communal labor but act as supervisors on work projects. Older women continue as members of the women's council in Amakiri, but in neither community do they play political roles comparable to the male elders. The majority of old women continue to be economically active, going to farm or to trade.

The accomplishment that brings most prestige to men and women is their ability to produce many children and to live to see the birth of a great-grandchild, or beyond. Their funerals are especially elaborate, including the performance of special dances and ceremonies. Grandparents receive slightly less elaborate funerals. In either case, the death of an old person with generations of descendants is celebrated and honored more than any other transition point in life.

■ 5
Relations between Generations

Every second week it is Timinepere's mother's turn to cook for Igbideh. In polygynous marriages in Amakiri, each wife in succession takes a week to cook and to sleep with the husband. Since Igbideh has two wives, Tubolayefa and Okubere have only a week off between these "shifts" which keep them and their children extremely busy. On this Wednesday morning Timinepere is dispatched to the father's room with a pot of tea and half a loaf of bread. She stays there while Igbideh eats, waiting for further orders. She says she dreads this chore; Igbideh is difficult to please and usually has a number of other requests that send Timinepere on errands all around the town and usually makes her late for school. But today he seems content as he drinks his tea alone while his daughter stands quietly in a corner. Timinepere returns to her mother's section of the porch, gathers the breakfast cups and plates, and washes them. Then she quickly changes into her school uniform and prepares to leave for school. Her mother stops her, however, and gives her instructions about preparing the midday meal which Timinepere will have to start after she returns from school. Tubolayefa will be away fishing today since Igbideh requested fish or meat for his meal. Besides, her family can use the cash that the sale of extra fish will hopefully bring in. It will be Timinepere's duty, therefore, to make sure that the younger children are fed, that the father is waited on, and that Ebimieowei and Tarere do the chores required of them. Even though she is only thirteen years old, being the eldest girl means that she is her mother's primary help and responsible for running much of the household. After school lets out at three o'clock, Timinepere rushes home and devotes the rest of her afternoon to doing household chores. By six o'clock she is done with cooking, feeding, bathing her baby sister, Jenny, and overseeing the cleanup activities of the two older children. As she prepares to go out and look for her mother, who is hawking fish on the back road skirting the compound, Igbideh summons her and sends her to meet an "uncle" (a classificatory brother of her father) who has just arrived from Port Harcourt. The man holds a salaried job as a government clerk. When he returns to Amakiri for family meetings, he wields considerable power due to his affluence, which includes the ownership of a two-story house in Port Harcourt and a car. Igbideh hopes to send some of his children to board with him in town while they attend higher schools. His arrival, therefore, usually causes quite a flurry as children of all ages are sent to wait on him. Although Timinepere does not consider him to be her specifically selected sponsor, she helps her two brothers carry in the guest's bags and prepares his bathwater. She cooks and serves his evening meal with much the same respect as she gives to her own father.

A few compounds away Omiebi Odozi is making fire for boiling water for tea. His sisters, Evelyn and Hope, are busy preparing their father's breakfast. The younger children are scurrying around under the directions of the mother, sweeping the porch and running for water. Since Benson is monogamous, Christiana and her children are responsible for taking care of his needs every week. This amount of work is counterbalanced by Benson's relatively larger contribution to the household budget. This morning, as almost every day, he gives cash to Evelyn so that she can go and buy meat at the daily market by the Government Watersite. While Evelyn runs off to the market, Benson sits down to drink his tea. This morning he motions Ebi to come and join him and directs Hope to bring another cup for her brother. This is a rare honor since the boy is only fourteen years old. As he is Benson's eldest son and primary heir, and since he is approaching puberty, he is gradually being taken out of the children's work group and treated as an adult male. Omiebi sits in respectful silence a few feet away from the father, but he seems pleased to leave when it is time to go to school. As the other children also prepare to leave, Christiana reminds the girls of work to be done in the afternoon and admonishes the younger boys to be attentive in school, while Benson reminds Omiebi of the mathematics quiz that will be given after the morning break.

When Omiebi returns from school he is free to settle down to his homework since there are usually no adult demands placed on him. The cooking is done by the girls and the cleanup by the younger children. The only chore he is occasionally asked to do is to run errands at the request of Benson or one of the other senior males in the family, such as F.O. or Sunday. These errands usually consist of delivering messages or serving drinks to visiting dignitaries. While these requests are fairly rare, he knows he must respond immediately in order to establish a proper relationship to the senior members of his family and to demonstrate the respect due from a junior to his elders.

PATRILOCALITY AND THE MATRIFOCAL HOUSEHOLD

In Amakiri the patrilocal extended family is the most immediate set of kinsmen who live in the same dwelling or compound. In Ebiama the comparable units of kinsmen living together tend to be ambilineal in that members trace their descent, and thereby their legitimate claim to their residence, through either male or female ancestors. Despite this difference, the two communities are comparable in the value they place on patrilocality. Children should live in their father's residence, and following marriage males should continue to do so while their sisters move out to join their husbands. The rule is simply more consistently met in practice in Amakiri than in Ebiama.

The two communities are also similar in the importance they give to kinsmen related to each other through their mothers. These uterine ties hold more opportunities for Ijo in Ebiama than in Amakiri, since inheritance and certain other rights and obligations are defined matrilaterally in the former, but they are not insignificant for the latter. Those who have married and moved to Amakiri, and therefore are not members of the patrilineage, provide the intimate linkage between full siblings. Women who are patrilineally related are considered to be as equally powerful as men in their ancestral capacities. Moreover, many women return to their paternal compounds when they are older or if they are divorced or widowed. As far as training for the future is concerned, youngsters are just as dependent on women for assistance in schooling as they are on men.

Most important in early as well as latter life are the full siblings, who, with their mother, are a nodule within the polygynous family. These matrifocal units are physically represented in living arrangements as we described them in the last chapter. They may occupy separate rooms in one compound or each occupy a separate house. It is here that everyday life unfolds, where the first sense of identity is evoked. In Ijo one always speaks of siblings using descriptive terms that indicate whether the relationship is through the mother alone or the father too. To be half siblings by sharing only a father is more important in Amakiri than in Ebiama, but there is no question of the solidarity and support that stem from having the same mother. The importance of this matrifocal unit is manifested in the competition and occasional conflict among the nodules of a polygynous family.

Kin relationships that extend beyond the physical dwelling place to form a descent group are seen as the link to the past and to the future. Membership is important here too for defining an individual's identity and for defining the persons most likely to be of help in times of need. In Amakiri and Ebiama the descent groups are large, and many members reside far beyond the compound or even the quarter. Those who have left, either temporarily or permanently, usually renew their influence each year when they return for a family meeting, for the town festival honoring the ancestors, or for funerals. Within this group, rank is presumably based on seniority. The most elderly males are honored, but men with wealth and successful careers are assuming increasing respect in the families and hold the highest positions of authority in the eyes of the youth.

Most of the fathers of our subjects in Amakiri are the heads of their compounds and therefore in positions of authority over the people residing there, but they are still too young to occupy positions of seniority within the family. In Ebiama, where the living arrangements are more diverse, out of thirty-nine households only half of them (twenty) contained the fathers of the youth we studied. In the other nineteen cases the head of the household or his wife was related to the father or mother of the youth. The children of the household heads' daughters also were found in four of these cases. The difference in household composition, however, does not diminish the importance of the father or his surrogate as the one who is supposed to preserve the peace by being impartial or uninvolved in the compound's day-to-day problems and affairs. Male heads of households are authority figures requiring respect from their wives and all the children living there. Often they spend more of their time outside the household with men of their own status than interacting with members of their family.

Obedience and Respect: Father-Child Relationships

When fathers were asked what they expect from their children, they invariably answered in terms best translated as obedience and respect. Obedience means children should perform any service they are asked to do, such as running errands, serving meals, waiting on visitors, and doing jobs around the house. Boys are also expected to pay attention to their schoolwork and to pass their exams. Girls should too, but they are also expected to work more around the house. Respect means not answering back to older males, greeting older individuals first, and maintaining a diffident attitude when addressed.

These expectations are mirrored in the children's statements as to what they should do for their father that would be considered good. In Ebiama, even though the adult male occupations thought to be of "traditional" importance are losing the interest of adults as well as the young, males are still engaged in these occupations to the extent that they are mentioned as part of expected activities. An obedient son in this context is one who follows his father to the bush, to farm, or to tap palm wine.

Expectations differ for males and females, and for older and younger children. Girls and prepubertal boys big enough to work around the house (beginning around six years of age) are at the beck and call of all males in the family. Older boys are considerably freer and are treated more as adults. In general, for boys, growing older means relief from service and strict obedience, whereas for girls it means the opposite.

Even though children may voice what they believe is the right occupation to which they should aspire, neither parent nor child clearly perceives the results of schooling, the particular occupations for which one is being prepared. Obviously, however, they are not farming, fishing, or palm wine collecting, and therefore a man is unable to teach his son the skills he will probably need for his future occupation. With their sons spending most of their time in school, and in Ebiama, at least, where many do not even reside with their fathers, fathers in general ignore the daily life of their children. Nevertheless, there is no lack of male surrogates. Even in households headed by women, male kinsmen residing nearby in the quarter play a role in guiding and correcting the behavior of their younger relatives. The evidence for male identification can also be seen in the response to questions about sex-role preference, referred to in the last section in this chapter. Males almost invariably prefer their own gender without preferring their father's occupational status.

The obedience and respect expected from children are inculcated in various ways. Younger children of both sexes are often physically punished. It is not unusual for parents to whip boys and girls as young as five and as old as fourteen years of age. Other senior members of the family may also beat children if they are insulting or commit a serious misdeed, but this punishment is rare by the time the children reach puberty. Another punishment frequently described by children is verbal abuse. As the children get older, displeasure is communicated by other means. The most effective of these is the threat not to help with the child's education by buying books or school uniforms unless the child behaves. To the extent that the child sees schooling as important, the threat may work. If the youngster does not consider education to be significant, the father has little leverage and may resort to sending the offender away to stay with a relative, hoping that he or she will reform.

Most youngsters seem to realize that it is in their best interest to remain in the good graces of their father and other senior kinsmen who may be in a position to help them in the future. Even though males will inherit their share of the joint inmovable property and girls can always look toward securing their future by marrying, most young people today are looking for a different kind of security in their adulthoods. With the introduction of universal free education and especially with the coming of secondary schools to both Ebiama and Amakiri, the possibilities for advancement and for opportunities beyond the limits of the towns have become realities. How many of the youth will avail themselves of these opportunities remains to be seen. What is important now is that most of the youngsters want to continue schooling and intend to secure good jobs and positions. For this they need help, and for this help they are dependent on either their parents or their parents' siblings, with more emphasis in Amakiri on the father's siblings and in Ebiama on the mother's. Because usually there are far more children in a family than potential sponsors, school-age children are often kept in line by competition for the goodwill of kinsmen who are successful or influential men. When their strategies pay off, the older children in a family are sponsored by the father, or a father's brother, or a mother's brother, and they in turn help their younger siblings. The father-son relationship by all accounts should be the strongest tie of all relationships, but even fathers admit that whereas sons might respect and obey them, they love their mothers most.

Love and Care: Mother-Child Relationships

While future prospects and past opportunities to a large extent are determined by one's membership in the descent group, a child's daily schedule and well-being are dependent on the group centered on the mother. The mother is the operational head of the household, its director and taskmaster. The ages of the mothers of our subjects range between thirty and sixty, with most of them in their late thirties. By the time their oldest children reach puberty, these women may have had four or five additional children. They are extremely busy and hardworking individuals who take care of the feeding and everyday needs of their children, in most cases with little financial help from their husbands. In monogamous families the situation is somewhat different, but even here providing daily food is not considered to be the husband's responsibility. The majority of the mothers are farmers who also fish and engage in some petty trading. Having had little schooling, they define a successful life for themselves in terms of advantageous marriages and many children.

It might seem that because the women carry the major share of the burden of feeding and clothing the children, they would want fewer of them. This is not the case, however, since a woman's prestige is assured and increased with each additional child. In Amakiri, children, especially sons, represent shares in the undivided patrilineal inheritance. Co-wives therefore compete against one another in producing sons, thereby gaining more voice and more economic shares in the family estate. In both communities children mean economic advantages for a woman. They contribute labor to her activities, without which she could not be as productive in farming, fishing, and caring for subsequent children.

Because of this dependency, mothers expect a great deal of help from their children. The majority of the children from about age six or seven on, therefore, toil at some chore when they are not at school.

The mother or her eldest unmarried daughter oversees this work force. Enforcing compliance is not always easy. Mothers cuff and hit the younger children as they try to punish some misdeed. They scream at the older children and threaten them with expulsion, which is an idle threat since children know that for their daily sustenance and well-being they need to live in the household. The mother is not perceived as such an all-powerful figure as the father, but her authority within the living unit is recognized and respected. She determines what children do day to day, and while many of them try to avoid hard work and complain about her requests, they generally comply.

Like fathers, mothers say that children behave well when they obey and do what is asked of them. The children say they act accordingly to avoid physical punishment and verbal abuse. Most of them also mentioned "love" (tare) and food as reasons for complying. Their mothers will love them if they perform their chores and assist their mothers in farming and cooking; their mothers will not feed them if they do not.

Although love is frequently mentioned as a reward and motivating factor for the relationship between a mother and her children, it does not prevent them from being openly antagonistic toward each other, much more so than any expression of hostility between fathers and children.

The intimacy between members of the matrifocal unit is much greater than that of any other unit in this society. It is a kind of intimacy that comes from sharing burdens and sharing space, but rarely from sharing thoughts and secrets. A mother does not usually talk to her children about their plans or aspirations, or about their progress or problems at school. Mothers teach their daughters how to perform tasks; they do not ask them for their opinions. Mothers are especially close in terms of cooperation with their older daughters, who are their closest allies in their everyday effort to subsist. Still, their relationship is largely pragmatic, limited to working together. As boys get older, they work less and less for the mother and they also move their sleeping quarters elsewhere. They still return to her house daily, however, for meals. When boys earn money from working in the bakery or collecting mangoes, they say they will give it to their mothers to buy food. None of our respondents said they would give their earnings to their fathers.

Despite the cooperation between mothers and daughters and the sharing of experiences as managers of households, they do not share an expectation of the kinds of occupations females will engage in in the future. Mothers allow girls to go to school, since they know that education is somehow important, but they will not make allowances for the time that school homework requires. Older girls are therefore expected to carry out the same tasks that their mothers did at their age. The consequence is that these girls essentially carry a double load, and very often education loses out. It also leads to frequent conflicts between mothers and daughters; mothers feel that the girls are not responsible and hardworking enough and daughters feel overburdened and pressured for time.

Gender Preference

In Amakiri, mothers and fathers agree that it is more important for a family to have boys since its continuity depends on them. In Ebiama, both sexes are equally stressed. Mothers, however, acknowledge the importance of girls as reliable hard workers. They talk about their daughters basically as helpmates who are there to assist them. Fathers talk very little about their daughters either in terms of the present or the future. Girls marry and raise children elsewhere and are effectively lost for the family.

While fathers and mothers both consider boys to be less responsible and less reliable than girls in their work performance, each has a different reason for wanting sons. Mothers think of sons as important in determining the quality of their old age and the amount of respect they may claim. Sons will continue to live nearby, support them when ill, and defend their interests. Should a woman get into a fight with a man, she can depend on her son to protect her. Perhaps because of this, mothers express a special love for their sons and admit to indulging them more than daughters. Fathers stress the importance of sons in making the descent group strong in the present and future. Because males are supposed to remain in the community after marriage, they are also thought of as a source of future support, despite the reality that many will reside elsewhere.

INDEPENDENCE AND RESPONSIBILITY FOR SELF

Responsibility training begins at the age of six or seven, when children of both sexes become an integral part of the mother's work force and realize that they are an important part of a group that shares the responsibility for the well-being of all members. Ijo believe that at this time children lose their special powers to transcend the worlds of living and dead (N. Leis 1982). As they grow older, they are not only given more work but become aware of their duties to the descent group and to the ancestors. Most of the time they are treated as independent agents who are expected to respond reasonably to the demands, or not at all. Adults are not surprised that children often bend the rules and avoid their duties, but children are still expected to behave properly. This results in a seemingly chaotic situation in which rules are poorly defined and children are inconsistently punished and rewarded. Whether a parent punishes a child often seems to depend on how swiftly the child runs away.

Attitudes toward independence are expressed in several ways. While children usually return home at certain times and eat with their siblings, nobody is surprised if they instead decide to eat elsewhere. They are, however, expected to do their work assignments, but here also they are often given some leeway as to the time this is done. Many of our adolescents had several places where they slept. The older ones especially often took trips to nearby towns, where they stayed with relatives for some days. Mothers, more than fathers, were aware of these absences but were not alarmed by them, assuming that the child knew what he or she was doing. Similarly, while the adolescents thought that parents approved of certain friends and disapproved of others, it made no difference in their choice of companions.

The sense of independence and responsibility for self that children learn early on is reinforced by their being treated to some extent as though they were adults. There is no separation of the spheres of adults and children. Even young children are allowed almost everywhere. They attend funerals and festivals that include dancing through the night, and since they have no private rooms they observe all public adult activities.

Becoming an adult by imitation and self-identification is not a simple process, at least as revealed by certain responses to the magic man interview, described more fully in chapter 7. In Ebiama we found that males identified with their fathers, as measured by responses to a set of magic man questions. Out of 20 responses only 2 males, one in the prepuberty and the other in the puberty stages, indicated that they would choose, if they could magically do so, to be a mother rather than a father. Their choice was consistent with their choices to be a girl rather than a boy. Females, on the other hand, gave a more mixed response. Three of 11 said they prefer to be fathers rather than mothers, and more than half (6) said they would change themselves into boys. They explained their choices by saying males are stronger and can better protect themselves.

In Amakiri, out of 13 boys who responded to the magic man questions, 12 chose to be fathers, and of the 15 girls, 11 chose to be mothers. The 4 who chose the opposite sex gave reasons similar to those in Ebiama. Additional interviews in Amakiri revealed that for boys and girls the most important person in the family is most frequently the senior male member of the extended family. They respect the senior male member or the father most. They also expect help with their career, education, and future from the father or from his seniors in the patrilineal family, although as we saw earlier, they love the mother most. The true seat of the Amakiri boys' identity is the patrilineal extended family, and as they grow older it becomes increasingly important. Boys talk about their duties and obligations to the entire group, including ancestors, and the responsibilities for property management that they will inherit as adult members. They recognize, however, the importance of the matrifocal unit in day-to-day responsibilities and profess loyalty to the mother and her interests.

In conclusion, the relationship of our young people to the parental generation is made up of a complex set of relations in which they are bound to a number of different individuals but yet maintain a high degree of autonomy. They are dependent on and have certain expectations of a variety of others, yet do not identify exclusively with only one particular person. This is partially due to the complicated nature of their family composition and conflicting loyalties between the paternal and the maternal groups, and partially to the fact that neither the boys nor girls growing up today have occupational role models among members of their parental generation.

◼ 6
Relations with Peers

SIBLINGS

The Amakiri Girls Secondary School lets out at noon, and Timinepere is usually at home by half past. On this Friday, on the road that fronts the Ekberi compound, she finds her mother selling the fish she caught in the morning. Tubolayefa is glad to see Timinepere approach and shouts at her to hurry and change her clothes. She wants her to take charge of her smaller children. Kemepuado, five, and Jenny, two, who are underfoot and who need to be washed and fed. Timinepere runs into her room and after carefully folding the blue and white school uniform, puts on her faded wrapper. She wishes she had time to take a bath to wash off the dirt of the road, but this will have to wait until the late afternoon when most of the people, including the small children, take a nap.

She picks up Jenny and, with Kemepuado trotting after her, carries her into the compound's courtyard. With the children running around, she lights the fire under the cooking pot to warm up their food. While it is warming, she picks up Jenny and draws her into a corner of the yard where she quickly washes her. After Jenny, it is Kemepuado's turn. Timinepere, however, discovers that she has run out of water. She shouts for her younger brother, Ebimieowei, ten, to go to the tap and finds that he has run off to play. Frustrated, Timinepere is looking around for some other child to send out when her sister Keyinmo, thirteen, the daughter of her father's brother, Blessing, appears from her kitchen and offers her a bucket of water. Timinepere is grateful but not surprised. Of all her sisters living in the compound, Keyinmo is the closest to her. In the afternoons when both of their mothers are out selling, they work closely together, caring for the younger children and performing most of their household chores. Washing, chopping, pounding, and child care are much easier when done in unison with a sister who is the same age and who can be trusted to help out in a pinch.

Omiebi arrives home from Okosibo Secondary School around one o'clock. He finds his sisters Evelyn, Hope, and Tubolayefa already busy chopping vegetables for the afternoon meal. Christiana, his father's wife, shouts at him to hurry up and change from his school uniform. Oyindeyinfa, age nine, arrives at this point with a bucket of water, which he drops by the older children and then runs off to play. Benson arrives and, after he has taken his bath, Evelyn serves him his meal as he sits alone on his porch, watching people walk by. The rest of the family, including mother and the seven children, eat together by the kitchen. After the meal is finished and the girls start washing the dishes, Ebi and Oyindeyinfa go down to the river to bathe.

Oyindeyinfa learned to swim from Omiebi at age five, but he still prefers to accompany his older brother whom he admires and respects. Omiebi is flattered by this and acts as protector and tutor to the younger boy. After their quick swim in the river they return to the house where Victor, their thirteen-year-old brother, the son of Benson's brother Sunday, is waiting for Omiebi. He wants Omiebi to accompany him to Ogboware quarter where he has been sent with a message. The two older boys set off, talking and laughing, but Oyindeyinfa will not be left behind; he tags after them, and soon the older boys call him to come along and join them. He runs up to Ebi, grabs his hand, and happily walks by his side.

The most important long-term relationship for youth in Amakiri and Ebiama is the one between siblings. Most of the members of the big multifamily compounds are considered classificatory brothers and sisters, some of whom are full siblings, others are half siblings, having different mothers and the same father, or different fathers and the same mother. The Ijo extend the terms for "brother" and "sister" to include all parallel cousins, descendants of brothers and of sisters of the same generation, even though they can be differentiated in formal terminology. In many instances siblings live elsewhere, and those at home come and go, but this does not diminish the importance of the sibling tie throughout an individual's life.

Regardless of the kind of sibling ties and whether they are full or partial, our subjects stress that they are all "blood relations," meaning they are all descended from the same person, at some point in time, and therefore inalienable and significant people. Brothers and sisters can be turned to for help and have a claim on one's time and resources. Brothers and sisters are expected as a matter of course to educate the younger ones in the family, and a successful man in a high-status position can be expected to be the object of attention of children of less affluent family members. Similarly, women who are in a favorable financial situation readily take on the education and care of younger family members.

Nevertheless, children and adults recognize different degrees of closeness between siblings. The closest tie is between uterine brothers and sisters, or between children of the same mother. The next is between coresidents of a compound who usually share membership in the patrilineal descent group and may be children of the same father or of brothers, and, finally, between members of the descent group, most of whom are not local residents, but are related through a distant ancestor.

The core group of siblings who have the most intimate relationship with each other consists of the children of one mother. She feeds and clothes them, and can order them around. In turn, they owe primary allegiance to her. Adolescents may work alongside and help the children of other mothers, but other mothers cannot assign tasks to them and only rarely discipline them. Depending on the relationship between co-wives, children may occasionally eat from the cooking pots of their mother's co-wives, but this is not usual. Consequently, children of the same mother usually form a solidary group that is slightly antagonistic to other similar units with whom they share a father. While they feel responsible for the welfare of all their father's children, they will most likely help educate their full siblings before any of the others. After the mothers' death, her private property is divided among this group, with the senior son usually presiding over its distribution. In Amakiri, women can be far wealthier, because of their trading activities, than in Ebiama. There is usually an understanding that boys have priority over immovable property, such as houses and stores, particularly if these are in their paternal quarter, and girls, who are usually married by this time and live else-where, over jewelry and cloths. If there are adolescents or school-children in the group, much of the property may be earmarked for their education.

The patrilineal emphasis in Amakiri results in brothers residing together in the same compound or in ones immediately adjacent to each other. As described earlier, the living options in Ebiama are more varied. Moreover, the extended family tends to be better defined in Amakiri than in Ebiama because in the former, adult sons of one father and all their offspring use the same patronym, which at this point seems to have stabilized at using the name of the grandfather as a last name. In Ebiama, two naming patterns coincide. One is like Amakiri's; a second is an adaptation of the traditional form of single names whereby, for example, Peter's son John is called John Peter, and John's son Bill is named Bill John. In either case, children who grow up in close proximity and are of the same appropriate age spend much of their time together working, studying, or playing. Boys and girls of the same compound who are sent to the river to wash clothes, or are told to chop vegetables, try to coordinate their schedules with that of their brothers or sisters. They share in watching and tending younger siblings and in running errands for the adult males. When they reach puberty they very frequently share sleeping quarters with an age-mate of the same sex from the compound and may help one another in procuring dates or sexual partners. As they grow older, these ties become increasingly significant, especially for those males who continue a lifelong coresidence and share in the management of family property. These individuals become the local representatives of the wider descent group and as such serve as the caretakers of family interests and property.

The most widely encompassing tie is the one between members of the descent group which includes "brothers" and "sisters" who are related through a distant ancestor. Nevertheless, they are still counted as members of the family and participate in honoring the common ancestors. They also partake in decisions that affect the whole group. In addition to building plots within Amakiri quarters, male members of sublineages inherit equal rights to farmland, lo-cated outside of the quarter. These large tracts of farmland, which often include fishing sites, are the common property of the patrilin-eages or segments of them and are annually or biannually appor-tioned at "family meetings" to members, or to members' wives who will do the farming. Since many of the men have moved to urban areas or have taken up nonfarming occupations, there is more available farmland than claimants at this point, so the division of land does not result in conflict or rivalry. Land disputes are frequent, however, between members of different lineages whose lands adjoin. The resulting fights and court cases often serve to solidify further the tie between the members of the patrilineal descent group. Other inherited rights include membership in the family council and the service to the paternal ancestors, as well as the responsibility to marry a widow.

Unlike in Amakiri, land is individually owned in Ebiama and inherited matrilaterally, except in the case of children of big-dowry marriages. Women obtain farmland from their mothers, or from their husbands, if they have moved to Ebiama. Land in the past was plentiful in this area for the same reasons it was plentiful in Amakiri; also compared to Amakiri, land disputes are no less frequent. Boundaries are often poorly marked, and their placement must be recalled years later since fields are allowed to lie fallow for long periods, sometimes a decade or more. An increasing population has resulted in the establishment of a new quarter subsection at the end of the village (P. Leis 1982).

In both communities any member of the descent group may ask permission to put up a building on plots around his father's compound or, as a more recent development, on land specifically set aside for this purpose by the family, as the area around the original site becomes overcrowded. The allocation of these plots and the jockeying for desirable locations are at the root of potential problems since the plots are much desired by all male members, even those who are not permanent residents during most of their lifetime, but who want to return to the town to retire and eventually to be buried in their own compound.

Whether distantly related siblings have an effect on an adolescent's life depends on their ages and their residence. If they live in Amakiri or Ebiama, their presence becomes quite significant: boys think of these more distant "brothers" as potential allies in schoolyard fights and in games; older girls may utilize slightly younger "sisters" to fetch and carry for them. Males can recruit sisters of all ages to serve them on special occasions. Even if they are not residents, members of the descent group assemble in the town for funerals and many attend the annual town festival—at Christmastime in Ebiama and in

Amakiri in the spring for the seigbein. These meetings, while brief, reinforce their ties.

In the relationship between individuals within all these groups, age and seniority are extremely important considerations. As with the adults, males have more power and authority than females, and seniority likewise commands respect and obedience. Thus, a senior girl has more authority than a junior boy, when he is young, but less than a senior boy at any time. A junior girl is definitely at the bottom of the heap, running errands and carrying loads for the others. To what extent individuals are able to enforce compliance depends on past considerations of rewards or punishments. In general, younger siblings respect and obey older ones, especially older brothers.

The relationship between siblings who are far removed in age resembles the one between children and parents. The older child is a caretaker and taskmaster whom the younger one looks to for help and for whom he or she has to work. The older children, on the other hand, even boys, are often very affectionate and patient with the young ones. The relationship between middle children who are close in age is somewhat more difficult. Since they are more or less agemates, it is difficult to establish a ranking among them, which results in a melange of cooperative, competitive, quarrelsome, and joking behaviors.

Sisters

Of all relatives, girls have the closest relationship to their sisters. This is especially true of daughters of one mother who share in the responsibilities and chores of their own small domestic unit. Sisters who have different mothers but the same father, or who are daughters of brothers and live in the same compound, are also frequently very close, especially if they are age-mates. They spend much of their time together, toiling on similar tasks and under the thumb of the same set of male authority figures. Although girls of the same mother recognize a special connection with their own sisters, daughters of an extended family share similar constrictions and opportunities. Sisters of similar ages are not often in the position to help one another with their futures, and their relationship is of a different nature. It centers around work and their common daily chores in which they cooperate. Their shared activities are usually economic in nature, and they recognize in each other a close ally in their obligations.

Mothers and daughters also have a cooperative working relationship, very similar to those of sisters, but a major difference has emerged in the present generation. In past generations, mothers served as role models who transmitted all their accumulated skills to their daughters, who continued their lives much along the same lines. In this generation, mothers are only partial role models in that they still teach the girls the skills necessary for a housewife, but beyond this they are unable to serve as examples to their daughters who are literate and preparing for a future more dependent on education. It is now the older sister's role to act as a role model and to help and support a younger girl in her efforts to combine these two careers. This makes the relationship between sisters of different ages important. The older girl supports the younger one, who in turn respects and obeys the other. Because of the financial strain that higher education represents for the family, girls usually have less opportunities than boys to continue schooling beyond the secondary level. When a female, particularly a uterine sister, is successful at obtaining gainful employment, she may be called on to sponsor her younger sisters with financial assistance by at least providing them with room and board.

When asked in the long interview, "Whom do you feel closest to in your family?" twenty of twenty-five girls in the PSU in Amakiri said their sister. On a related question, nineteen of the girls said that they would "turn to the sisters for help" and twenty-two that they would "get advice with schooling and education from their sister." When asked "What do sisters do together?" all twenty-five girls said that they help one another, in work and with their future plans as they grow up. In Amakiri, sisters are not rivals for inherited wealth. They do not inherit patrilineally, and the stakes in the mother's property are usually small. Whatever wealth the mother has accumulated is shared by her children according to seniority, and, as previously mentioned, girls generally receive such portable property as jewelry and cloths.

In Ebiama, this question in long interview was asked differently: "Would you rather have a brother or sister? Why?" None of the girls or boys picked a sister. Of the sixteen girls replying to the question of what kind of help they would seek from an older sister, eleven mentioned money, food, or clothing; four said they would go for advice or for assistance when sick or lonely; and one astutely observed that if her mother was dead she would go to an older sister to ask for farmland. Should sisters continue to reside in Ebiama following their marriages, they would share their mother's farms. We did not find any expression of competition or jealousy between sisters, because, they claim, there is sufficient farmland.

The relationship of sisters, whether of similar or of different ages, lasts through life even though they usually marry away from the quarters or even from the town. Sisters, including those of the same father only, travel to each other's towns, often bringing many of their children along on extended visits. Children of sisters living in different parts of the country know each other and are sent to stay with their aunts. The bonds between sisters are similar in practice in both Ebiama and Amakiri, but because children of sisters belong to different patrilineages in Amakiri, the relationship between their children usually does not last beyond the lifespan of their mothers, whereas in Ebiama the tie may continue in the ambilineal descent group.

Brothers and Sisters

Ideally, brothers should be protectors and helpers of their sisters, regardless of their age. Sisters. on the other hand, should serve their brothers and respect them. In reality, the brother-sister relationship depends much on their respective ages, and there is considerable variation in the resolution of these ties.

Older brothers generally receive the expected respect from their younger sisters. They in turn protect and help them. Older girls, however, because they often serve as mother surrogates, expect obedience from their younger brothers but do not always receive it, especially as the boys approach twelve or thirteen years of age and are increasingly released from their household chores. The result is a great deal of fighting and yelling, with the older girl usually losing out. Brothers and sisters of similar ages also quarrel because their closeness in age makes clear-cut ranking difficult.

In the postpubertal years, the lives of teenage brothers and sisters become increasingly separate. Girls continue working around the house, whereas boys are released from these chores and spend little time in the compound. As previously mentioned, our spot observations indicate that beginning around twelve years of age girls were observed working three times as much as boys and playing half as much.

Brothers may be aware that their sisters have boyfriends, but the siblings' social lives are separate from each other. Once the girls marry, an important difference between Amakiri and Ebiama becomes apparent. In Amakiri, girls marry and move away, even though they remain members of the patrilineage and occasionally come to visit the parental home. Their brothers show little interest in their lives even though they profess a continuing responsibility for their futures. Nor are brothers generally involved in educating their sisters since they tend to focus their attention on their younger brothers. The exceptions to this observation are some much older brothers who are successful professionals in the cities and who may occasionally sponsor a younger girl's education, usually as a form of repaying a debt to the girl's father. Hoping for this, whenever such an affluent individual visits Amakiri, adolescent girls vie for his attention and try to serve him. In general, in adulthood the lives of brothers and sisters of whatever age settle down, and we see respect on the part of the sister to the brother who has become an adult male member of her patrilineage. At no point of their life cycle is their relationship an especially close or intimate one.

In Ebiama the brother-sister relationship is of more significance, though not necessarily more intimate, than in Amakiri because of the matrilateral emphasis given to inheritance and to residential choices. The mother's brother retains legal rights to his sister's children, and they in turn see him as a potential sponsor for their schooling. In the Ebiama interviews, of the nineteen male responses to the question of which sibling they preferred, only two said they would choose a sister; the same response was also given by two out of eighteen female respondents. None of the boys or girls stated that he or she would prefer an older sister to an older brother. One reason given for not wanting sisters was that they marry and leave. Girls wanted an older brother to defend them or their fathers, or to help by giving them money for food, clothing, and books. Almost all the boys say they would go to an older sister for food. In the Amakiri interviews, only two boys claimed that they feel "closest to" their sisters. Both of these sisters were much older and acted very much as surrogate mothers. Fifteen girls said that the person they "most respect" in their family was an older brother. Only three girls and four boys said that a sibling of the opposite sex "helped them most" or "shared with them most."

Brothers

Brothers of all ages recognize a special tie to one another which transcends the present and connects them to their ancestors, as well as to their future descendants. Sons of different mothers, however, may have somewhat different loyalties and interests.

During prepubescence, brothers share in each other's workload, much as sisters do. Older brothers help and direct younger ones and try to get them to wait on them and serve them, with somewhat mixed results. By and large, the juniors respect and obey the older brothers, but those of similar ages often quarrel and fight. As they become older, the boys increasingly divorce themselves from the lives of the women and spend much of their time with one another. It is also at this point in the life cycle that older, grown-up brothers assume a special importance. Since few fathers have occupations their sons want to imitate, older brothers serve as role models or as sponsors for their younger brothers. Boys assume that one of these brothers will help them with their education or with finding jobs, and look toward these individuals as possessors of skills they want to acquire.

The brothers most likely to help one another initially are sons of the same mother. Their solidarity with each other continues until all the sons are grown up and their future is ensured. After this, especially once the mother has passed away, it is the patrilineal tie in Amakiri that takes precedence over the uterine tie to the same mother, and male lineage members of different mothers and different generations treat one another equally. In Ebiama the strength of the sibling connection through same mothers or same fathers will depend on where the siblings choose to live. Brothers who live together have the strongest tie, and those with the same mother are stronger yet.

The importance of this tie, which continues through the life of an individual and beyond, cannot be overemphasized. Even if adult brothers live apart, they still consider themselves natives of Amakiri or of Ebiama and maintain houses in the town. They share in the ownership of family property and participate in town festivals and in honoring the ancestors. Adult males of a family also participate in the family council and make decisions that affect all their children. The personal relationship of most brothers continues as a close and supportive one throughout their lives. When brothers do quarrel, it is considered bad, but not unusual. As mentioned in chapter 1, fraternal conflicts are the legendary basis for the fragmentation and resettling of many Ijo villages. Brothers can claim each other's help as a matter of course, and those who do not oblige are ostracized and criticized. Having many brothers can be a burden or a blessing, depending on one's status and achievements, but having no brothers is a dire fate for an Ijo to imagine.

Of twenty-five Amakiri boys interviewed, twenty-two felt "closest to" their brothers. All of them said that "brothers help the most" and that "one depends on brothers the most." Twenty said that it was "their older brother they respected most." However, only ten younger boys said that it was their brother whom "they worked with" and who "helped them in their chores." Twenty-two of the boys, on the other hand, respected older brothers most; none of them said their sisters. In Ebiama, twenty boys wanted an older brother, and two had no preference between a brother or sister. Brothers were preferred primarily because they could protect the younger sibling in a fight. Brothers were also seen as a source of help in providing money for food and clothes.

FRIENDS

Every morning on her way to school, Timinepere passes by the Okreke compound where her best friend, Felicia, waits to join her. Felicia is the oldest daughter of Paul Okreke, a trader, who lives with his two wives and seven children in a large compound by the "back road" on the opposite side of Makido from the Ekberis. Felicia has three older brothers who are away from Amakiri, either working or schooling, and at fourteen she is the oldest child still at home. Her younger siblings keep her constantly busy, and she has little time for play. She is a serious girl who shares Timinepere's interest in studying. The two have been friends since the previous year when they started secondary school.

This morning, as usual, Felicia is standing by the road as Timinepere arrives. The two set out together, joining the hordes of blue-uniformed girls walking north toward the girls' school. In the opposite direction a gray-uniformed procession of boys and older girls passes them on their way to Okosibo Secondary School, as well as an even larger crowd of smaller children in green, also going south to the primary school. Timinepere and Felicia walk close together, talking and laughing, but keeping a wary eye out for boys or children who may try to play pranks on them. This walk to school is one of the few opportunities for the girls to get together without younger siblings to watch or some chore to do. Consequently, they try to leave early and walk slowly in order to prolong the time for gossiping. Today, Felicia is telling Timinepere that their age-mate, Lois, has been seen going around with a boy, which at fourteen is still considered unusual and therefore newsworthy. As they reach the school, Timinepere suddenly remembers that she missed geography and history yesterday because she had to take her mother's yams to market. She reminds Felicia of her promise to lend her the notes from the class. Felicia reassures her that the notes are complete and gives them to Timinepere to copy in the ten o'clock break.

Omiebi also walks to school with his best friend, Bernard Otutu, but this is not their favorite time together. In the evening, after the Odozi family has finished its meal, the plates have been washed and stacked, and the porch swept, Omiebi slips away from his younger brothers and walks down to Bernard's house. Bernard, the son of an Isoko trading couple who set up a small food store by the "back road," is fourteen years old, the same age as Omiebi, and they are also in the same class at Okosibo Secondary School. They have been friends since the previous year when they transferred to Okosibo from the primary school. Prior to this, Omiebi's best friend was John Oseke, but the two had a bad fight when John refused to let Omiebi listen to his new radio. Bernard and Omiebi say they like each other because they can count on each other's support in fights and because they like to do the same things.

The "same things" consist primarily of sitting around Bernard's father's store in the evenings, waiting for customers, and playing records or cards in the meantime. Other boys stop by, come in and talk, then leave. Bernard's younger brothers and sisters run in and out. As it gets dark, Eunice Otutu, his mother, closes the store and takes the smaller children off to bed. Bernard and Omiebi can now "stroll out" or walk up and down the "back road," watching boys of their age also going around in twos or threes and older boys and girls passing by as couples. Bernard and Omiebi are not interested in girls yet, but they have great fun watching couples on the road. Around nine o'clock Omiebi suddenly remembers that he has homework for the next day. He boxes Bernard affectionately on his back and heads toward home.

Ijo society is not based on associations with permanent membership, nor do the Ijo recognize age-grades or age-sets in the sense conceived of in many other African cultures. In the past a sense of association for the purpose of sharing food existed among those born at approximately the same time, particularly if one of the members was a hunter and he brought home an animal he had killed. Despite the lack of formal groupings, the age principle is important and relative age is used to distinguish between individuals. Young people of similar ages face similar sorts of expectations from adults, which in some contexts makes them close allies. As a consequence, friendship, referred to as *toiwei* in the Ebiama dialect and as *ekeyei* in Amakiri, is usually formed between individuals who are close in age.

The friendship tie among our subjects usually is intense but not enduring. While two individuals are friends, they provide strong mutual support and spend most of their free time together relaxing and having fun. But the relationship is impermanent and shifts as rapidly as the children themselves from place to place. A friend in primary school is usually not a friend in secondary. Interests and loyalties change; individuals quarrel. This fact does not diminish the importance of these ties, however, while they exist. Friends share intimate thoughts and emotions with each other and are allies in facing the social world made up of other young people. Friends are important in the learning of values and in gauging oneself against age-mates in a situation not primarily devoted to the serious matters of work and family survival, as it is usually with siblings.

Even though personal choice is stressed in the selection of friends, certain general characteristics of those who choose to be friends can be noted. During the entire span of the adolescent period, friends are individuals of the same sex and of similar age. Frequently they are neighbors or live nearby, which makes interaction easier. Children who eventually become friends have usually known one another all their lives, but their intimacy starts in school where they attend the same class. They sometimes get to know one another through participation in the church choir or attendance in a religious sect, such as the Seraphim and Cherubim. Friends are usually not close kin, especially not those siblings who live in the same compound. Coresidence and friendship seem to be mutually exclusive, although more distant kin may become friends.

Because there are few visitors to Ebiama, almost all friendships are drawn from the Ijo population. In Amakiri, on the other hand, there is a considerable amount of moving in and out of the community by Isoko and Urhobo traders, by children who are schooling here with relatives, and by those who are sent out to school in a city.

Newcomers encounter few difficulties in meeting others once they start attending school. In this, they are also helped by the transitory nature of the friendship tie, which makes fitting in relatively easy.

In their definition of friendship, respondents of different ages used quite similar criteria. Without exception, they all emphasized the difference between friends and siblings: brothers and sisters are for life, they are the same "blood," whereas friends are those people whom you like and who are similar to you in taste and temperament. They should be there when you need them; they are those with whom you do things and who do things for you. These expectations are somewhat different for younger and older youth; the younger ones consider friendship in instrumental terms, what friends do for one another: loan money for school lunches; lend pens, pencils, and schoolbooks; help out with schoolwork by sharing notes when one of them is absent. They also spend their free time together and have fun. Younger boys especially stress the value of friends in assisting in fights and quarrels with others. Younger girls, on the other hand, emphasize that friends do not lie to one another.

Older subjects, in addition to practical support, also talk expressively about each other. They say that friends give advice to one another and try to correct each other's mistakes. They also gossip together but not about one another. Girls find out about menstruation from friends. Boys help one another arrange dates and will make their rooms available for a friend's sexual encounters. Older boys also stress the importance of friends as helpmates in fights.

Of whatever age, none of them seems to think of friendship as a lasting tie. Friends are for coping with problems and situations in the present. One needs a friend as a sort of protection against the outside world. Protection includes information gained through gossip, warning, and good advice as well as actual physical help in fights and providing more tangible items such as loaning money and books, all of which are generally in short supply in the household.

Even though the concept of friendship seems to remain similar through the pre- and postpubescent years, there are obvious differences in the activities that friends engage in at different ages and in the criteria used for selecting friends.

Peer groups are important as play groups even in the earliest school years, but the earliest friendships that our subjects recall were formed in primary 5 or 6, or around ten or eleven years of age. Eight- and nine-year-olds do not yet consider any other child a particular "friend." Children of this age have play groups and walk to school with crowds of other children from the same or from neighboring compounds, but the notion of a special sharing relationship with an unrelated person has not yet entered into their lives. They tend, however, to limit their groups to same-sex individuals. There is a recognition that boys and girls, while they may do the same household chores, have basically different interests and like to spend their free time in different activities. Girls of this age like to play a game of ludo (a game resembling hopscotch) on the main paths or inside the compounds. Boys play ping-pong in Amakiri; in both towns they play drafts (checkers) and football (soccer). The earliest friendships evolve from these play relationships when children realize the importance of one special ally and helpmate. By the age of ten or eleven they walk to school with a special "friend" and play ludo or football with this person. They also join together to watch their younger siblings and to run errands.

As we saw earlier, by twelve or thirteen years of age the work activities of boys and girls begin to diverge, affecting their social activities and the nature of the time they spend with their friends. Another factor that further separates boys and girls in the twelve-to-fifteen age range in Amakiri is the separate secondary schools for boys and girls.

The activities of girlfriends in the twelve-to-fifteen age category tend to be more work related than that of boys. They try to coordinate the timing of those economic activities that take them outside of the compounds, such as washing clothes on the riverbank; in Amakiri they also go to buy or sell in the market. Girlfriends walk to school together, offer to help each other in school, and spend their free minutes in each other's company. These girls consider themselves too old to play ludo, and play cards or listen to records. In Amakiri there are no public spaces where girls can hang out. In Ebiama the main paths running through the village are the public gathering places. At those rare times when young teenage girls are not occupied with a household task, they gather in small groups at benches along the paths to talk and to watch people walk by. The "back road" in Amakiri is not considered appropriate for girls this age since strolling there has certain sexual connotations. The riverbank is the playground for younger boys. Girls sit around in stores, but these are usually owned by the parents of one of them and as such are private spaces where one enters only by invitation.

Girls in this age-group tend to interact in small groups. They no longer have play groups nor do they have organized sports. All the twelve-to-fifteen-year-old girls in our study had a "best friend" with whom they spent their free time. They were cliquish and usually gossiped about others.

Boys in the twelve-to-fifteen age-group have a much wider geographical range from which to select friends than do girls. Since boys are increasingly less burdened with economic chores, they are free to range away from the compounds and to pursue other interests. These boys participate in many large-group activities that involve some sort of organized sport, such as football or track and field at the school compound. They also participate in activities with smaller groups, such as going on fishing or hunting trips. Boys in Amakiri can also attend the movies when they are shown in a room behind one of the local bars. They are usually so rowdy while watching the films that girls' parents prohibit them from going. Moreover, boys this age can and do "stroll out" on the back road. While they do this with same-sex age-mates, they are clearly observing dating couples and learning from their examples. What work-related activities they do together tend to be limited to sitting in a friend's parents' store and assisting the friend in selling.

Although these boys move around in larger groups than do the girls at the same age, they all have and readily name their best friend. Without such a person they think that life is unsafe since one is unprotected in case of a fight, which is an ever-present possibility. Members of this age-group seem to be in frequent violent physical encounters of shorter or longer duration. While girls also hit each other, the level and frequency of aggression is much higher among boys. The cause of a fight is often unclear: fights erupt for no apparent reason in the course of walking to school, playing games, or simply going by the store of another boy. These are the times when friends step in and either join one of the combatants or try to separate them.

By the age of sixteen, the behavior of the girls resembles that of adult women. They are hardworking, serious, and responsible individuals who have taken over running a household from their mothers. "Best friends" are still other girls. It is other girls they confide in, whom they need to advise them, and with whom they work and share their aspirations. When men and boys begin to interest them, it is considered appropriate for these girls to accompany one another to dances in order to meet males. While these girls may go to dances and "stroll out" with boys of similar ages, their sexual partners are usually somewhat older males. Sexual relations will be further described in the next chapter.

For boys sixteen years of age and older, same-sex friendships also continue to be important. These boys are now free of any obligation around the house and are expected to focus their attention on their education and future plans. While some of them do study, it is rare to find one in this age-group who takes schoolwork seriously. Most of these boys spend much of their time "strolling around," looking for girls, goofing off, playing records, and acting macho. Some of them have part-time, after-school jobs in construction work but this does not prevent them from playing around in the evenings. They usually join with male friends who come over to the compound or with whom they go walking around. Sometimes girls also participate, and there is a great deal of teasing and noisy merrymaking. These boys are generally not old enough to attract a steady girlfriend or a permanent sexual partner, but they engage in sexual activities whenever they can; for this they need the help of male friends for introducing them to their sisters, carrying messages, and loaning their rooms. In general, same-sex friendships at this age seem to be more intimate and supportive than those with members of the opposite sex, although relations with the opposite sex become increasingly important.

By the end of their teen years, or in their early twenties, many of the girls in Ebiama and Amakiri are married or have children and tend to concentrate their attention not on friendships but on their families. Most of the boys have left town, having moved to larger cities for either education or employment, separating from their friends of the earlier years. As they grow into adulthood, these young men also increasingly turn their attention to their family responsibilities. It remains to be seen whether this pattern, established by the previous generation, will continue with the current one where the age of marriage and the assumption of familial responsibilities are delayed because of the increasing opportunities for education for both sexes.

SIBLINGS AND FRIENDS: COOPERATION AND CONFLICT

A peer group is made up of a complex set of relationships that may be sorted into two basically different categories: those between siblings and those between friends. These two categories have much in common but also differ in some significant aspects.

Friends are most often the same age and the same sex; siblings usually are of different ages. Friends are together and help one another because they are similar and have much in common. Siblings who are closest in age often quarrel, whereas those of different ages cooperate best. One helps those siblings most readily who are most different in both sex and age; those siblings who are most similar engage in rivalry. As a consequence, expectations from siblings and friends are different. A friend is for now—for the everyday sharing of tasks and pleasures, for help and protection in fights, and for the testing of one's position in the social world of peers. Games and fun are with friends. While friends may share economic activities, this is not done to share the workload itself, but to spend time together.

Siblings are forever. Relationship with them concerns the family and the lineage, its past and future, for which they share the responsibility. While there are different degrees of commonality between siblings related to various degrees, the overriding fact is the common descent which ties them all together. The emphasis is on responsibility to one another and to the group as a whole, not on liking one another. When siblings work together, they share the load, not only the pleasure of spending time together.

■ 7
Gender Preference and Sexuality

Achievement of adult sexuality and reproductive capacity is the hallmark of adolescent development. The biological and physiological changes bring about an awakening of sexual interest in individuals. In so far as we can understand the interaction between biological changes and psychological ones, complex behavioral adjustments require new self-images and role requirements. It is generally agreed, even by those who stress the significance of genetic codes, that the expression of these biological and psychological changes is shaped by the sociocultural context. This chapter describes sexuality in the context of Ijo culture and society, including attitudes toward sexual behavior and sex-role preferences, and ideas about the self and others as masculine and feminine beings.

SEX-ROLE PREFERENCE

The concept of sex-role preference here refers to an individual's preference for either the male or the female role in terms of overt behavior. This preference was examined using four interview techniques: the draw-a-person test, the magic man interview, a semantic interview, and an intensive interview on gender identity.

The draw-a-person test was given to fifty youngsters in Amakiri and thirty-one in Ebiama with the primary aim of noting which sex

TABLE 7.1

Draw-a-Person Test

	SEX OF FIRST DRAWING	
	MALE	FEMALE
Male informant		
Amakiri	16 (75%)	6 (25%)
Ebiama	18 (95%)	1 (5%)
Female informant		
Amakiri	13 (49%)	15 (51%)
Ebiama	9 (75%)	3 (25%)

was drawn first and the degree of sexual differentiation between male and female drawings. The test was administered in the two communities by the researchers with the help of opposite-sex assistants. In Ebiama we also asked those who participated in this test to tell a story using the figures they had drawn. We assume that the first drawn figure may be an indication of sex-role preference, as would be the contrasts that might be found between a male and female figure. While the first of these produced results that could be quantified, the latter was difficult to interpret. For the most part, the sexual differentiation of the figures was limited to drawing males in long trousers and females in skirts. Very few subjects drew any other gender-specific paraphernalia, such as earrings, hats, or hairstyles. There was very little difference between male and female subjects in this respect. None of the subjects in Amakiri drew male sexual parts; the majority of the males drew female figures with clearly defined breasts, but none of the females did. In Ebiama none of the boys or girls drew female genitalia, but one girl and several boys drew male figures with exaggerated penises, in proportion to the bodies. They gave no explanation in their stories for drawing these sexual features, apart from acting amused at what they had depicted. The lack of sex differentiation in most of the drawings seems to be accounted for by inexperience with drawing itself and by the girls' modesty and reluctance to approach the subject of sex openly.

The results of identifying the sex of the first drawn figure are given in table 7.1. As the table shows, most of the boys and girls in Ebiama drew a male figure first and a female figure second, whereas in Amakiri a majority of the boys drew a male figure first and more than half of the girls drew then own sex first. These data are not statistically significant when interpreted by a correlation measure, such as chi-square, but the tendency of Ebiama boys and girls to prefer the male role is consistent with the findings reported in the previous chapter on sibling preference and in our subsequent measures on this subject. The preferred status accorded females in the test responses in Amakiri also coincides with the economic and political achievements of a number of women in Amakiri in both the marketplace and in their community association.

Of the six boys in Amakiri and the one in Ebiama who drew a female first, five, including the one from Ebiama, were in the third, or final, stage of their pubertal growth spurt. The other two were fourteen-year-olds in the second stage of their growth spurt. A possible interpretation of their responses is that what the draw-a-person test elicits from these pubertal and postpubertal males are sexual fantasies or a preoccupation with sex.

The magic man interview (described in chap. 3) is a test for identifying family role preferences, including sex and age. The results are summarized in table 7.2. Twenty-eight youngsters (13 boys and 15 girls) in Amakiri and 39 (21 boys and 18 girls) in Ebiama participated in the test. The responses of both sexes were similar in one major respect: males want to be males, and a goodly number of females would just as soon be males too.

Respondents made this clear when in answer to the question of whether they would like to be reborn as a boy or a girl, all the boys in Ebiama replied "a boy," and 12 of the girls gave the same reply. Only 3 girls said they wanted to be "a girl;" 2 did not reply, and 1 said either sex. In Amakiri, boys indicated a preference for being boys, with half of the girls wanting to be girls and the other half boys.

Sex preference was somewhat more ambiguous in response to the direct question of whether the respondent wanted to be a boy or girl: in Ebiama two boys said they wanted to be a girl; six girls said they wanted to be a boy. In the choice between boy or baby and girl or baby, in both communities half the girls chose "boy" and the majority of girls picked "girl," indicating a preference for the older role. The boys, however, picked "baby," indicating that the baby could be male. In contrast, when deciding between boy or baby, only one male informant in each sample picked "baby," whereas the female informants were about evenly split between "baby" and "boy." It seems clear that whereas girls frequently choose male roles, boys wish to avoid the female choice, even at the price of selecting a very young role of unassigned gender.

TABLE 7.2
Role Selection for Magic Man Interview

INFORMANTS	AMAKIRI ROLE SELECTED		EBIAMA ROLE SELECTED	
	Father	Mother	Father	Mother
Boys	12 (92%)	1 (8%)	19 (90%)	2 (10%)
Girls	4 (27%)	11 (73%)	6 (40%)	9 (60%)
	Boy	Girl	Boy	Girl
Boys	12 (92%)	1 (8%)	19 (90%)	2 (10%)
Girls	4 (27%)	11 (73%)	6 (40%)	9 (60%)
	Girl	Mother	Girl	Mother
Boys	6 (46%)	7 (54%)	7 (35%)	13 (65%)
Girls	6 (40%)	9 (60%)	12 (75%)	4 (25%)
	Boy	Father	Boy	Father
Boys	4 (31%)	9 (69%)	11 (48%)	12 (52%)
Girls	5 (33%)	10 (67%)	11 (65%)	6 (35%)
	Girl	Baby	Girl	Baby
Boys	3 (23%)	10 (77%)	8 (38%)	13 (62%)
Girls	13 (87%)	2 (13%)	13 (76%)	4 (24%)
	Boy	Baby	Boy	Baby
Boys	12 (92%)	1 (8%)	20 (95%)	1 (5%)
Girls	7 (47%)	8 (53%)	8 (50%)	8 (50%)
	Reborn Boy	Reborn Girl	Reborn Boy	Reborn Girl
Boys	12 (92%)	1 (8%)	15 (100%)	0 (0%)
Girls	8 (53%)	7 (27%)	12 (80%)	3 (20%)

The answers to the other questions in the magic man sequence differed in the two communities. With sex held constant there was no clear preference for an older role in Ebiama, whereas in Amakiri both boys and girls preferred the older role to that of their own generation.

The intensive interviews on gender identity were conducted in Amakiri with 8 boys between the ages thirteen and eighteen and with 7 girls between the ages of twelve and eighteen. In Ebiama 19 youngsters were comparably interviewed—5 girls, twelve to nineteen years old, and 14 boys, twelve to eighteen years old. In general, the boys were open, frequently amused at the questions, and showed little reluctance in talking about private or sexual matters. All the Ebiama girls and the majority of the girls in Amakiri, however, were embarrassed and displayed a great deal of difficulty in talking about these subjects. The following excerpt from an interview with sixteen-year-old Daniel Adoni in Amakiri is fairly representative of a boy's responses to our questions:

▪ INTERVIEWER: *Now I want to ask you some questions about the differences between males and females. First of all, how do you know that you are a man?*
DA: *Because I have got all the qualities of a man. I am capable of marrying and sexing my wife.*
IN: *Do you think it feels different to be a woman?*
DA: *Yes. There is a great difference. The physical building of the body, sexual parts, and the ability to conquer fear. Men are more courageous.*
IN: *Now, lets talk about girls in general. Do you like or dislike them in general?*
DA: *I like girls in general. They are hardworking, keeping the house clean when they are married and taking care of the children.*
IN: *What do you like best about girls?*
DA: *Their shape.*
IN: *Do you like girls who show off?*
DA: *No. If she tries to show off, I will show her down.*
IN: *Do you like girls who quarrel and fight?*
DA: *No, because they cause a lot of problems.*
IN: *Do you like girls who act like boys?*
DA: *No, they are not supposed to behave like a boy; they are not qualified to do what boys are doing. Boys are people who love doing rough things, like fighting, using bottles and those dangerous tools in fighting. If girls do that, they can get easily wounded because they don't have power.*
IN: *Do you think girls should behave different from boys?*
DA: *Yes. The ways boys behave, girls don't behave like that. I like girls who are cool, that is, quiet.*
IN: *Would you rather study, play, or work with boys or girls?*
DA: *With boys, because we can learn from each other but not from girls.*
IN: *Can you describe your ideal girl? How would she behave?*
DA: *She helps me at home, helps my mother to wash plates, she must serve me the way I want. She greets me every morning. She must be obedient not only to me but to my brothers and to her elders and to respect them.*

IN: *Have you ever thought that you might like to be a girl?
Would you like to be a girl?*
DA: *No. I don't want to be a girl. I like the way I am. Girls have
to work hard, help around the house, and I don't want to have
that thing they have every month.*

There was unanimous agreement among all the boys participating in the intensive interview regarding this last question. All stated that they preferred to be a boy and gave similar reasons: girls had to work harder, boys were much freer. Only a few of them mentioned the physiological difference.

In general, the boys presented a picture in these interviews of extreme gender-role differentiation. Their preference was for girls who are quiet, obedient, respectful, and hardworking. Their image of boys was of tough and courageous beings, and they preferred working, studying, and playing with their own gender. As a boy in Ebiama summed it up: "We don't like to play with girls, they always bring misunderstanding; we only marry them."

A similar gender-role differentiation appeared in the girls' interviews, as seen from the following excerpt of an interview conducted with sixteen-year-old Regina Ekberi:

■ INTERVIEWER: *Do you think it feels different to be a woman than
a man?*
RE: *Yes. Girls have breasts, boys don't. If I were a man, I would
be more powerful and more proud.*
IN: *Do you like or dislike boys in general?*
RE: *I like them in general.*
IN: *What do you like about them best?*
RE: *I like those that are helpful. If they work, they help you with
money.*
IN: *Do you like boys who show off or those who fight?*
RE: *No, I like them best if they are quiet.*
IN: *Do you like boys who act like girls?*
RE: *They don't act like girls. They are not quiet and helpful.*
IN: *How do boys act?*
RE: *They behave different, they are more rascally, they smoke,
they fight and beat girls. The good ones will use these abilities to
defend you.*
IN: *How does an ideal boy for you behave?*
RE: *Like my brother Michael. He finished school and doesn't look*

for trouble. He protects me, I can go to him when I am in dif-
ficulties, he will listen and help. He is quiet.
IN: *Would you rather work, study, or play with boys or girls?*
RE: *I would rather work and play with girls, but I would study*
with both. Boys are smarter.
IN: *Have you ever thought that you might like to be a boy?*
RE: *Yes. I would prefer to be a boy. Boys have a better life.*

Four out of the seven Amakiri girls agreed with this last state-
ment, for reasons which included the following: boys have a better
life, boys are more free, and boys do not have to work so hard. One
of the remaining three girls said she wanted to remain a girl even
though men have an easier life than women because women do not
have to be as self-sufficient as men; they can marry if nobody schools
them. The responses were similar in Ebiama. Nineteen-year-old Betty
Isaacs, for example, one of the few who preferred being a girl, said by
way of explanation, "however bad or lazy I am someone will have to
marry me and feed me."

In general, the girls in Amakiri, similar to the boys, presented a
picture of gender-role differentiation. They considered boys to be
noisy, prone to fighting, and more powerful and proud. Girls were
more quiet, hardworking, and had a more difficult life. The majority
of the girls considered boys to be smarter in school and wanted to
study with them. The girls also looked for help and protection from
their older male siblings. The major difference between the boys and
the girls was in the boys' clear preference for their own sex role and a
desire by many of the girls for the opposite.

The young people's ideas about others as male and female beings
in their society were also elicited with the help of intensive semantic
interviews. Twenty of the subjects (ten males and ten females) in
Amakiri participated in this interview, which was based on the assignment of thirty-five personality descriptors, commonly used in the
Ijo language, to one of the sexes. The terms were originally elicited
from another group of informants who were asked to describe the
behavior of a bad/good man, woman, or child. The resulting thirty-
five terms were written on three-by-five-inch file cards and presented
individually to twenty of our subjects. They were asked whether the
particular term described the behavior or was more characteristic of
males or females or both.

There was almost unanimous agreement between the responses

TABLE 7.3

Male versus Female Traits

MALE			FEMALE
	0 ·	100	Sad, talkative, cowardly, shy, vain
	10 ·	90	Envious, silly, troublesome, wicked
	20 ·	80	Angry, playful, quarrelsome, lazy, harsh, nasty
	30 ·	70	Disobedient, liar, mischievous, selfish, stubborn
	40 ·	60	Happy, generous
Respectful, serious, striving	50 ·	50	Proud, pleasant
Gentle, clean	60 ·	40	
Kind	70 ·	30	
Quiet, honest	80 ·	20	
Calm	90 ·	10	
Clever, wise	100 ·	0	

of the male and female respondents, and their answers are therefore presented combined. The number of "male" and "female" answers were tabulated for each individual adjective. These numbers were then converted to proportions of the total number of answers given to that adjective ("both" answers were eliminated since they were very few), then scaled as shown in table 7.3. The adjective *angry* illustrates how the scale was constructed. Five informants said that the term characterized males and fifteen that it described females, therefore on our scale *angry* appears on the female end, the fifteen versus five responses having been converted to 75 percent female and 25 percent male.

On the basis of the clustering of adjectives, we divided the scale into three parts: those adjectives that were applied predominantly to males, those that described both genders, and those that applied predominantly to women. Both males and females were almost equally seen to be happy, generous, respectful, serious, proud, pleasant, striving, gentle, and clean. The adjectives that were considered to characterize females best included sad, talkative, cowardly, shy, vain, envious, silly, troublesome, and wicked. Males, on the other hand, were described as wise, clever, calm, quiet, honest, and kind. Somewhat surprisingly, many more adjectives were assigned to women (twenty) than to men (six), and while the female adjectives were negative, the image of women that emerges from these

TABLE 7.4
Male versus Female Traits in Ebiama

	BOYS	GIRLS
More intelligent		
Boys	13	4
Girls	1	11
Equal	4	0
No reply	4	2
More honest		
Boys	11	2
Girls	2	10
Equal	5	3
No reply	4	4

descriptors is more vivid than that of the men. The basically negative image of femaleness is in keeping with the data from the previously presented interviews.

In Ebiama, twenty-nine informants (fifteen females and fourteen males) were asked to characterize themselves rather than the other sex. We found that there is almost no difference in the terms used by either sex to describe themselves, except for one. More than twice as many boys as girls described themselves as "talkative." In Amakiri, both sexes agreed this adjective described girls exclusively. The adjectives used by at least 50 percent of the respondents to describe themselves, beginning with the most frequent, were gentle, calm, courageous, sympathetic, likes to joke, likes to play, talkative (males), generous, clever, and intelligent.

We then asked respondents in Ebiama to describe the opposite sex, using five adjectives frequently used in everyday speech to describe a person: strength, pugnacity, quarrelsome, intelligence, and honesty. Twenty-two boys and nineteen girls were in complete agreement on one adjective: boys are stronger than girls. Both sexes also largely agreed that boys fight more than girls and that girls quarrel more than boys. They disagreed almost completely on who was more intelligent and who was more honest (see table 7.4).

Girls, as in Amakiri, saw boys as being more intelligent when intelligence was defined as "performance in school," but not otherwise. Reference to honesty was also defined by informants in more than one way. To be honest means not to lie or to steal. There was general agreement that when it came to dishonesty, girls lied more than boys, and boys stole more than girls.

The projective tests and intensive interviews confirm the configuration of adult gender roles. We saw earlier that women play important economic roles in the society; they are involved in agriculture, fishing, and trading. They manage and are primarily responsible for the well-being of their own household units. The importance of these activities is recognized and valued but they are not held in high esteem. The economic roles men play produce more cash income than women, especially in Ebiama where women cannot participate readily in trading because of the absence of a local market. That their position is somewhat more advantageous in Amakiri, because of their marketing and trading success, is demonstrated by the higher preference given to women in the draw-a-person test, described earlier. Their economic power notwithstanding, women are the outsiders, even when they are married from another quarter of the same community, who must obtain their residence from their husbands; in large part in Ebiama, and exclusive in Amakiri, they obtain their farms from their husbands as well.

Highly esteemed positions in Ijo society were traditionally and continue to be in the hands of the males. All of the political affairs of both communities are conducted by the men. In Amakiri, where a political hierarchy has been in place for a much longer time than in Ebiama, the pere, the supreme ruler of Amakiri, has always been a male. In the Western-introduced national political system, males similarly dominate: all the elected representatives from Amakiri and Ebiama are males.

A new path to high-status positions is available today to either sex through education. Males and females are encouraged to take advantage of these opportunities; however, as we saw earlier and will see in the next chapter, the sexes have differential chances for success. Girls are still burdened with household chores and have less time to study. Although they work very hard at both, and might even perform better than boys in school, many of them eventually become pregnant, drop out of school, and end up leading lives similar to those of their mothers. Since both men and women agree that women work harder than men in traditional roles, and since the opportunities for females to acquire new roles are severely constrained, it is not surprising that both boys and girls prefer the male gender role.

SEXUAL ACTIVITY

Children grow up surrounded by others of all ages and both sexes. In the course of their daily life in a large compound they see small children running around naked, observe them being bathed, and in their early years play with others in the nude. Most children gain their first knowledge of anatomy in mixed-sex play groups between the ages of four and six, during which period the little clothing they wear is easily abandoned. There is no prohibition of sexual play in this age-group, and informants recount tales of games in which little boys compare penis lengths and examine the anatomical difference in little girls.

Children and adolescents alike are aware of the nocturnal activities of their parents. In polygynous compounds there is open talk about which wife's turn it is to spend the night with the husband, particularly since cooking for the man and sleeping with him are associated activities. Part of the burden of cooking falls on the adolescent girls since they must help their mothers. There is also a great deal of joking and bantering that goes on among the women when there is a new wife who is desired nightly by the husband during her week of cooking. Infants are usually delivered at home, and the birth of a new baby may be observed by adolescents and discussed by children of all ages. The result is that sexual activities are not taboo subjects, and sexuality and reproduction are part of the daily routine of living. This does not mean that sexual acts are performed in the open or indiscriminately. Quite to the contrary, sex among adults is a private act, jealously guarded, and if observed, the adults would be embarrassed and offended. Nonetheless, when a four-year-old imitates the movements he saw his father performing the night before, adults shriek with laughter. Sex for the Ijo does not appear to be hedged with guilt and sin, compared to the dictates of the Judaeo-Christian heritage. If individuals have an improper sexual relationship, such as an adulterous one, and they are caught, the husband would beat his wife or demand that an adultery fee be paid. In the case of incest, or having sex in the bush or directly on the ground, it is left to the ancestral spirits to punish the guilty, and they are made to pay a fine or sacrifice a chicken to placate these spirits.

Interest among adolescents in members of the opposite sex begins around fifteen or sixteen years among girls and around the same age among boys. While the majority of the youngsters' activities in these ages are still performed with others of the same sex, there is a growing awareness of the other sex. Girls in this age-group spend much of their time working together with one or two others of similar ages and, in their free time, playing around the house of one of their girlfriends. Fifteen- or sixteen-year-old boys, when not engaged in organized sports, roam the town in groups, looking for something to do. Meeting with members of the opposite sex usually occurs in this context. A small group of boys starts hanging around a particular compound where girls work or play together. To begin with, the boys stay on the periphery, bantering and joking with the girls. Eventually, they begin to participate in the girls' card games or simply sit around and talk with them. In time, individuals begin pairing off and walk off together. It is said that girls in this age-group are extremely shy and that it is usually the boy who makes the initial approach. This is often done through an intermediary, usually the boy's friend or the girl's brother or older sister. This person asks the girl to come away from the compound since there is "somebody who wants to talk" to her. The girl, amidst a great deal of giggling and feet shuffling, follows. The intermediary may also approach the girl in school, or on the road coming or going to school.

After a young couple's relationship is established, changes in their behavior are noticeable only to their best friends. The routine of their daily life continues much as before, working and playing in groups, mostly with same-sex friends. These youngsters are considered to be too young to be openly "strolling out," going to dances, or having sex. Their private interactions are limited to occasional meetings behind a friend's compound or to encounters at the waterside after dark. Much of the secrecy that surrounds these sexual activities is due to the disapproval of the parents, particularly those of the girls. While this may seem contradictory to the openness with which sex is discussed and treated in general, parents say they disapprove of sexuality in their pubescent children because of fear of a daughter's early pregnancy (Hollos and Leis 1986).

When the girls reach fifteen or sixteen years and the boys seventeen or eighteen, their sexual behavior changes. The secret petting behavior gives way to genital intercourse. None of the boys interviewed in this age-group claimed to be a virgin, and while the information on girls' activities are more indirect, it appears that most girls past the age of sixteen have engaged in sexual intercourse. The evidence on girls comes from statements made by their boyfriends, by their girlfriends, by their parents, and, most objectively, from the frequent pregnancies encountered in this age-group.

Boys speak more freely about their sexual behavior than do girls; whether they are truthful is difficult to ascertain. The following is a taped interview, conducted by a male research assistant in Amakiri, with eighteen-year-old Okubotin Fiya.

■ INTERVIEWER: *How did you first find out about sex?*
OF: *I talk to my friends about it. We were joking and talking about some type of words and this came up. They told me that the first time when you have sex, the body will shock you, just like an electric shock.*
IN: *Is this what your friends told you?*
OF: *Yes. And its true, it will shock you.*
IN: *What about your father? Did he ever talk to you about sex?*
OF: *No, it is not his business to talk to you about sex.*
IN: *Are you interested in girls?*
OF: *Yes, I am interested in girls.*
IN: *How are you interested in girls?*
OF: *I am interested in playing with them and sexing them.*
IN: *When did you start this?*
OF: *Well, it was with one of my sisters, with my father's brother's daughter. At that time I was ten when she started fooling with me. But it wasn't until the age of fifteen when I knew what she was doing.*
IN: *What about your friends?*
OF: *Most of them start moving with girls in form 2. When they start, they play, they say, go and hide. Hide and seek. Then they run to such secret places and start fooling around, touching.*
IN: *How old were you when you actually had sex with a girl?*
OF: *I was seventeen. That was quite late. Before then, I was having girlfriends but I had no chance to do anything with these girls.*
IN: *Where do people your age do this?*
OF: *I do it in my own house because I am staying in my uncle's compound. Others do it in a friend's room usually when the other boys sharing the room are away.*
IN: *Do they arrange this, to be away?*
OF: *Yes, the other boys will go stay somewhere else.*
IN: *Do they ever do it in the girl's compound?*

OF: *No, it wouldn't be right.*

IN: *How about in the bush or in the school compound?*

OF: *(Laughs) No way.*

IN: *Do you think that your father knows that you are having sex with girls?*

OF: *Yes.*

IN: *How about your mother and your brothers?*

OF: *Sure, they all do.*

IN: *Are boys discouraged from having sex before they marry? Or is it OK for boys to have sex?*

OF: *Once I am up to age, it depends on me. There is no real specific age that this is. Boys who want to, can engage themselves in sex.*

IN: *Do you think girls are as interested in having sex as boys are? Or is it different for girls?*

OF: *It is about the same. Some boys are interested in sex; it is just the same vice versa—some girls are equally interested.*

IN: *Is it OK for girls to have sex before they marry?*

OF: *Yes, nobody will say anything. But some girls have some type of sexual sickness, anywhere they go, they like to have sex. Any minute, any time they must sex. If they don't sex, there is something going wrong. This is not right; a girl should not freak just anyhow.*

IN: *What do you have to do to get a girl to have sex with you?*

OF: *Have to talk to her, spin her. If the girl likes me, she will agree. Maybe give her mineral and tease her, trying to make her happy.*

IN: *What if you get a girl pregnant? What would happen?*

OF: *She would have the baby.*

IN: *Do you know of anybody, a boyfriend or a girlfriend to whom this has happened?*

OF: *Yes. He went to the parents of the girl to make up all the requirements necessary for the girl's circumcision. The parents accepted the boy as their in-law.*

IN: *How did the parents feel about this?*

OF: *His family was happy, they took the baby and raised it.*

A similar interview with a small sample of girls produced much less open information about the interviewee but provided indirect data on other girls' sexual behavior. The following interview was conducted with sixteen-year-old Regina Ekberi.

■ IN: *How did you first find out about sex?*
RE: *In school people joke about sex. Then we had biology in secondary school. Children are not allowed to watch people have sex.*
IN: *Did you ever discuss sex with your friends?*
RE: *I have heard my friends gossip about others who have boyfriends.*
IN: *Did you ever talk to your mother about it?*
RE: *No, my mother never told me about it. She warned me though not to move with boys when I was younger.*
IN: *Are you interested in boys? Do you go around with a boy yet?*
RE: *I don't go around with boys as dates. I have many friends, schoolmates, they come around and we joke. But I don't stroll out.*
IN: *What about most of your friends?*
RE: *Girls in my age-group many of them have boyfriends and have sex with them. About half and half. They do it in secret. The parents want the girl to finish school first. They usually find out about it when the belly starts to show.*
IN: *Is sex something that is not allowed to girls in your age?*
RE: *Because the parents want them to finish school.*
IN: *Do you think that girls and boys are equally interested in sex? Or are boys more interested in it?*
RE: *Boys are more interested in sex. Boys hang around you, buy you drinks.*
IN: *What happens if a girl gets pregnant?*
RE: *The parents may beat her but at the end they are happy to have the baby.*
IN: *Do girls get abortions?*
RE: *No, once it happens it is best to keep the baby.*
IN: *Do you know any girl to whom this has happened?*
RE: *Yes, Lillie, a girl in my class. She dropped out of school and stays in her father's compound.*
IN: *Who is (paying for) feeding the baby?*
RE: *The parents to the boy and to her together.*
IN: *What do you think will happen to Lillie eventually?*
RE: *Maybe she will come back and finish schooling and marry later.*

Despite this seeming double standard for boys and girls, most parents are aware of the sexual activities of this age-group, and it is an accepted fact among the adults that a sixteen-year-old girl is probably engaged in these activities. A girl of this age is considered a young woman; she looks like an adult, she carries adult responsibilities, and the parents expect her to behave as an adult.

The mothers of this generation were married by age fifteen or sixteen, and most of them had had at least one child by the time they were seventeen years old. Mothers and fathers say that schooling is important, but when a girl becomes pregnant and drops out of school, they welcome her child. It appears that mothers, especially, consider childbearing to be a more normal destiny for their daughters than any other occupation.

The boys' parents have no objection to their sons' sexual exploits and usually welcome a child fathered by him as a member of the family. In Amakiri it is they who pay the circumcision fees and buy the appropriate gifts for the girl's circumcision, thereby affiliating the child to their patrilineage. In Ebiama, boys see their futures as somewhat imperiled by having a child because they might have to drop out of school to earn money to help support the mother.

Most young couples, despite parental tolerance, do not give public or open expression to their relationship. In part this reflects the Ijo behavior pattern of rarely showing affection in public. Physical contact and touching is more an expression of friendship among same-sex individuals. Males, for example, often hold hands as they walk around town. In contrast to this, during the entire research period no adults of the opposite sex were observed touching, holding one another, or kissing.

In those cases where the relationship becomes more serious and permanent, open involvement between the young people is expressed by the girl coming around to the boy's compound and cooking for him, just as a wife does in a polygynous household. Unless she is from another community, she continues living with her own parents and going to the boy's place only at mealtimes. If she is from elsewhere, at this point she is likely to move in with the boy and go to school from his house. In either case, they are now openly having sex, with the girl freely entering the boy's room.

This type of open expression of a relationship is rare in the age-group we are dealing with here. Most of these young people experiment with sex without entering into a permanent relationship. This is especially true for the boys for the entire age span in the study sample. Girls seem to share this attitude in the earlier age-group, but the older ones (seventeen and eighteen year olds) are beginning to look around for more permanent partners. These partners are most often not their age-mates or even the older adolescent boys, but somewhat older men, with whom a liaison or marriage will give security and status to the girl.

The age of marriage in this generation is delayed by both sexes' almost universal attendance, at least in the first years, of secondary school. Boys do not marry before their late twenties, when they have completed their schooling and have established themselves in some occupation. With the current economic recession in Nigeria, marriage is becoming more and more problematic and further delayed. As Amakiri males of previous generations migrated to nearby towns to look for employment, this generation of young males also leaves the community soon after completing school. In Ebiama the contrast between generations is sharper as many more youngsters than ever before now leave the community to seek work in urban areas. The youths of both places look in the towns for either work or further education. In any event, they are not available as marital partners to the young women who are looking for mates. The males frequently return to their home communities at a later age and, with the help of their male relatives, "look for an appropriate girl," who is preferably Ijo but not from their own quarter. By that time the girlfriends of their adolescent years are most often married or gone.

Some of the young women also leave town after completing secondary school and work or continue schooling elsewhere. They will often look for and find husbands where they are living, sometimes with the help of relatives and sometimes through chance encounters. Ijo mates are preferred but the major consideration is status, especially for the more educated young women, and it is not always possible to find Ijo males of appropriate education or background. The majority of young women, however, remain in their hometowns and find their husbands there. They graduate from the adolescent boy/girl dating and romancing to a more pragmatic search for an appropriate adult male partner.

Ijo marriage is a long process which is initiated and completed in a number of ways, during which the husband acquires different rights in his wife. In each case, parents emphasize that their children choose their own partners and establish their own relationships. The

definition of a "proper partner" involves the positive gender characteristics mentioned earlier in this chapter, as well as pragmatic considerations based on ethnicity, education, status, wealth, and reputation.

Before a girl finally settles down to a permanent partner and the
marital proceedings are initiated, she frequently bears a child. Under
the prevailing social and economic conditions in Nigeria, high fertility can be seen as an adaptive strategy for the majority of men and
women and thus the parents' attitude toward early sexual activity is
bound closely to the desire for large families. Our findings, then, contrary to cross-cultural hypotheses which have posited that complex
societies, such as the Ijo, would have restrictive premarital sexual
behavior, support Whiting's conclusion that there is *not* "a simple
linear relationship between restrictiveness and complexity" (Whiting,
Burbank, and Ratner 1986, 293).

From the men's point of view, additional offspring add to the
power of their descent group or family because prestige in Ijo society
is determined by the numbers of adult male followers a man can
muster. Males are also important because the strength of families is
derived from the support of sons who are placed in influential positions outside of the community. Men in these positions can help their
siblings or their brothers' children into similar positions of power and
wealth. Within the community, children are important in establishing
claims to landholdings in competition with other descent groups.

Females share this perspective on the desire for children. A barren woman in Ijo society is an unfortunate being. With children a
woman's prestige and value is assured and increased with each additional child. In Amakiri, children represent shares in the undivided
patrilineal inheritance. Co-wives, therefore, compete against one another in producing more sons, thereby gaining more voice and more
economic shares in the family estate. Each woman's group of children represents a unit in competition with other such units within
the polygynous extended family. For a woman who has not yet established a marriage, having a child is still advantageous since via the
child she can establish land claims to the child's father's family lands.
In Ebiama the basis for such competition is missing since inheritance
is conveyed through the mother. The desire for children, however, is
no less than in Amakiri. Three of the five girls responding to the
intensive interview said they want ten to fifteen children.

For an unmarried young woman, bearing a child therefore is not
unusual and far from disadvantageous, whether she later marries the

child's father or not. Approximately half of the sixteen-, seventeen-, and eighteen-year-old girls in our Amakiri sample became pregnant during the research period, and the majority of the other half the year after. In several cases, the pregnancy initiated the beginning of marital proceedings; in others it did not. In either case, the young mother acquired certain advantages: a share for her child (and therefore for herself) in the father's property rights (in Amakiri), and a proof that she is not barren. In Ebiama only one girl in our sample became pregnant during the year. She had not yet gone to live with her husband.

Becoming an adult Ijo woman is bound up with pregnancy. In Amakiri there is an added contingency to attaining adulthood—circumcision—which is avoided in Ebiama. In the former community women are circumcised in the seventh month of gestation, which is the first step in the ritual process toward the attainment of full adult status, culminating in later life in a "coming out" ceremony. Clitoridectomy these days is performed by a doctor or a midwife. The young woman returns to her father's home for the occasion, if she has previously married, where she is cared for exclusively by her mother. The operation, which is done under hygienic conditions, with a sterilized knife, is very small and its major importance is that it produces some bleeding. The wound is bathed and dressed for several days by the girl's mother, during which time she performs no household chores and rubs her skin with a red powdered dye. She proudly walks around the community, her skin color announcing the important process which she is undergoing. None of our female subjects, regardless of their future plans and aspirations, voiced any objection to the procedure, and most of them eagerly looked forward to it as to a graduation ceremony into adulthood.

The clitoridectomy fees are paid by the father of the woman's unborn child, which establishes the paternity of the child. The husband or boyfriend pays a fee to the midwife or doctor, gives a number of specified presents to the girl, and holds a small celebration in her parents' home. Men express pleasure at paying the expenses because this affiliates the child to their lineage.

Thus, premarital pregnancy is neither unusual nor disadvantageous for young women. The eventual goal, however, for all of them is marriage, whether they plan to continue their schooling or not. Pregnancy often is the first step toward attaining this status but not always.

As we said earlier, marriage is a process that consists of a number of steps, and it is difficult to state the point at which a couple is considered "married." A frequently occurring situation is when a girl becomes pregnant while living in her parents' home. The man responsible for the pregnancy, in the case of Amakiri, pays the clitoridectomy fee, but he does not thereby acquire all rights to the woman's sexuality or to her labor. Whether she moves in with him or stays with her parents, should she take a new lover he cannot collect adultery fees.

If bridewealth negotiations are under way, the girl often moves to the man's compound and may bear him further children before the payments are completed. In some cases the girl may refuse to leave her parents' home after the birth of the child and to contribute labor to the man's household until the payments are complete. Often she eventually marries someone else. There is no onus attached to her in this kind of situation, and many men claim that they prefer to marry girls who have already proven to be fertile. Even if the girl does move in with the man after the birth of the child, many of these relationships are fragile and she may leave with ease until the bridewealth is paid. After the fees are paid, the union is considered stable and the man has the right to the wife's labor and exclusive sexuality.

Not all unions are preceded by pregnancy. As we saw in the Ebiama PSU, the five married women in our general sample did not have children. In these cases bridewealth payments are made by the groom to the appropriate members of the bride's family, and a small ceremony consisting of an exchange of drinks between the families of the couple is performed. The bride then joins the husband. Some people claim this type of union is risky for the man, however, since the bride has not yet been proven fertile.

■ 8
Present Premises, Future Promises

PREPARATION FOR THE FUTURE: SCHOOL AND WORK

By half past seven on weekday mornings, Amakiri's back road swarms with schoolchildren in uniforms of various color. Students of the town's three schools are distinguished by the green (primary school), gray (Okosibo Secondary School), and navy blue (girls' secondary school) skirts and pants they wear to school. As Timinepere and her friend Felicia enter the blue-uniformed stream going toward GSS, they are passed by the gray and the green streams going in the opposite direction. Many of her brothers and sisters join these other groups and disappear in the general chaos and noise. Since the town has two thousand schoolchildren, who walk to school every morning and afternoon, the back road becomes virtually impassable to vehicles during these hours. The crowding of the roads is made even more severe by many children who, in addition to carrying their books and notebooks, also carry desks or chairs on their heads or machetes in their hands. The furniture is necessary because the schools are unable to provide sufficient equipment to accommodate all the children; the machetes are used to cut the grass and clear the school compound during work periods.

Timinepere attends form 2 in the girls' secondary school where she shares a desk with Elo Ofubu, an Isoko girl who is sixteen-years-old but has not yet passed the form 2 final examinations. In Elo's case this is not due to a pregnancy. She is sponsored in her schooling by her grandmother's sister, a trader, who is the widow of an Amakiri Ijo. When the aunt is away on buying trips, Elo stays at home and minds the store, so she misses approximately half of each school year. Timinepere is fortunate in this respect; her parents believe that education is important and none of the Ekberi children are kept periodically out of school to work. Timinepere wants to be a teacher. Her mother, Tubolayefa, agrees with this goal, but because of her own heavy burdens and her lack of understanding of the time required for schoolwork, Tubolayefa is unable to help her daughter in her attempts to do well in school.

As Timinepere and Felicia arrive at the school compound, they join their class at the morning assembly. This morning they arrive on time, before morning prayer. After assembly, the classes break up and go off to the classrooms. Since GSS is a small school, with a student body of around 150, this is a relatively quiet and orderly process. Timinepere has four classes today: arithmetic, English, geography, and social studies. In English there is a book report due today on a novel, *Things Fall Apart,* by the Nigerian writer Chinua Achebe. Timinepere is in trouble: every afternoon during the previous week she has tried to read the book, only to be interrupted by Tubolayefa or Igbideh sending her on an errand or by a younger brother who needed her help. Last night she was determined to finish it but fell asleep by the flickering kerosene lantern at nine o'clock. As the teacher admonishes her for her lack of preparation, she promises to do better next time. She is not alone; over half of the girls in her class were unable to read the book which is one of the required texts for the West African School Certificate exam, usually taken at the end of form 5.

Omiebi's path crosses that of Timinepere as he joins his gray-uniformed schoolmates on his way to Okosibo Secondary School. As usual, he walks with Bernard and two other boys from his class. For a short section of the trip the grays are vastly outnumbered by the green-uniformed primary school children who seem to flood the road from all directions and who dart in and out of groups, hitting and yelling at one another. At the center of the town the smaller children turn into their own school compound and the Okosibo students continue for another mile and a half until they reach their own destination. Okosibo is located off an unpaved road in a clearing in the middle of the forest. Since there are no school buses or public transportation, the walk may take up to an hour for children living in the opposite end of town. Even for Makido children who live relatively centrally, it is at least a half hour's brisk walk. The school's remoteness is used as an excuse for the chronic lateness of many students. Omiebi and his friends dawdle along the road and barely manage to sneak in and join their class before assembly starts. Those children who arrive late and are caught by one of the teachers are grouped together and made to kneel throughout assembly. Those who are considered incorrigible are sent to the principal's office where they are caned. These punishments notwithstanding, children come habitually late, move around and talk during assembly, and pay little attention to the teachers' admonishments. After assembly, the classes break up and, amidst a great deal of noise, fighting, and pushing, especially on the part of the younger children, go to their appointed rooms. Okosibo is a large school, with a student body of about five hundred. Forms 1, 2, and 3 are only for boys, whereas forms 4 and 5 are still coeducational.

Omiebi is in form 3, one grade ahead of Timinepere who is his age-mate. His father, Benson, decided that he was ready for school and insisted on enrolling Omiebi in primary 1 at age five, which is against the law, since a child has to be at least six years of age before entering school. Because birth certificates are not required, it is easy to lie about a child's age and enter him either early or late, at the parents' convenience. Omiebi passed his primary school final exam, and the exams in forms 1 and 2 in secondary school with good results and has been promoted to the next class each time.

This morning the first class is geography, followed by math, in which there is a quiz. Omiebi is well prepared for the quiz, primarily due to Benson's insistence on studying. Benson considers education to be of extreme importance for all his children, and especially for his oldest son; Omiebi does his homework conscientiously. Unlike many of his schoolmates, he also attends regularly. Omiebi says he would prefer strolling out or listening to records in the evening with Bernard, but there is not the slightest doubt in his mind that he will complete all five forms at Okosibo. He wants to be a teacher like his father, but with a higher degree which will qualify him as a secondary school teacher. He might even try to enter a university, provided he does well enough on his school certificate exams, in order to become a school principal. Graduating from a university would make him the first member of his extended family to do so.

School

The learning of skills and preparing for the future in traditional Ijo society occurred through intergenerational transfer. Young people learned the requirements of adult functioning in the society through observation and interaction with parents and other adults. This took place in the context of the household, and most of the skills the children learned were practical and applicable to the immediate context. Learning skills from parents and other adults ensured not only the continuity of traditional occupations but also reinforced a relationship in which the older person took the role of the expert. This was in keeping with the established system of authority which was based on sex and seniority, with elders (particularly male elders) wielding the most power. The introduction of formal schooling has gradually changed the educational system, with boys experiencing the change historically earlier than girls.

Schools were established in Amakiri and Ebiama at approximately the same time in the early 1900s by the Anglican Christian Missionary Society (CMS). The addition of a Catholic mission school in the 1940s in Amakiri was symptomatic of that community's more pluralistic composition. The aim of the missions was to promote conversion by teaching people to read the Bible. In Amakiri the first teachers were English missionaries and all instruction was in English; in Ebiama the teachers were Ijo converts from the eastern part of the delta who used a Bible that had been translated into the Nembe dialect of Ijo. The number of students in each village was small, and almost all of them were boys. Very few of them attended school beyond a few years of primary training, and even then usually only sporadically. During British rule, those students who wanted more schooling than offered at Amakiri or Ebiama (infant 1 to standard 4), had to attend in other communities.

Not until Nigerian independence was a standard 6 added to the primary schools and secondary school classes introduced in both Amakiri and Ebiama. The schools continued to attract children from the surrounding area where no schools or upper primary school classes existed. At the same time, as in the past, students wanting advanced classes had to attend them elsewhere. With independence, the schools were no longer directly controlled by the missions, but their influence was still felt because many of the teachers had been trained by them and religion was taught during school hours. Church services were held in the school buildings.

In 1955 the regional governments abolished school fees, resulting in a large upsurge of enrollment. By that time nearly all the male children of the two towns attended classes, at least for a few years, resulting in an almost universal literacy among men, albeit a minimal level for many. The enrollment among girls gradually increased after this date.

In 1957 the school system of the country was revamped. In place of the standard classes, the new system was split into primary and secondary schools, with six and five classes, respectively. The next year Amakiri received a "secondary modern school" which functioned until the mid 1960s. The modern schools were designed to provide three years of postprimary education to those children who did not gain admission into a secondary school, which was not completed until 1969. As mentioned earlier, Ebiama's secondary school had just reached the third level by 1982. In Ebiama the classes in the secondary school are referred to as "secondary school (SS) 1, 2, 3," whereas in Amakiri they are called "forms."

In 1976 the government of Nigeria launched a universal primary education program designed to provide free, compulsory primary education for all children of school age throughout the country. Teachers were also expected to have completed at least standard 6 for teaching in the primary schools, and teacher training school or university for teaching in the secondary schools. In both communities attendance rose dramatically. In Amakiri the two primary schools were merged to form one large facility, resulting in overcrowding and the need to conduct classes in two shifts for lack of adequate space. Primary school enrollment doubled, from five hundred to one thousand and the number of teachers rose from twenty-two to sixty. Although the numbers were smaller, the percentage of increase in Ebiama was similar. Girls began to attend in almost the same numbers as boys, including older girls who had missed enrolling when they were younger. The inflation of the numbers of primary school attenders eventually resulted in growing enrollments in the secondary school.

As a consequence, a girls' secondary school (GSS) was built in Amakiri in 1980. In part, the GSS was perceived as a sign of the growth and development of the town, since in larger towns, like Warri, schools were sex segregated. Its construction, however, was due to a decision by the Bendel state school board that the educational goals and requirements of female students are somehow different from those of males. Since girls have less time to prepare their daily homework and many of them drop out at least for a while after form 2 or 3, it was felt that boys could progress better if they were segregated from the girls. The GSS in 1982 has only forms 1, 2, and 3; girls in forms 4 and 5 still attend Okosibo. While many of the GSS students are of the appropriate ages for the lower grades, there are several older girls also in attendance. Most of the older girls were formerly students at Okosibo and dropped out after becoming pregnant, so the student body at GSS partially consists of nursing mothers. Others have been withdrawn by their parents for some years, in order for them to help around the house or with marketing. GSS is considered to be an inferior school to Okosibo, with less qualified teachers, lower expectations for the students, and lower average test scores.

The three schools in Amakiri and the two in Ebiama are built in a similar style and consist of a number of low buildings made of concrete blocks, with corrugated iron roofs. The schools are located on land at the far end of each town, where available land was to be found. None of the buildings in any of the schools is quite completed to the point of being painted on the outside. The inside paint is peeling and dirty; the floors are gray concrete. Classroom furniture is scarce; there are not enough desks or chairs for all the children, who must either double up or carry their own chairs to school. In the Amakiri secondary schools the science equipment has never arrived. In Ebiama the microscopes are set out for use, but the school lacks a qualified teacher. Books are in short supply because they have not been provided by the regional governments. Other supplies, such as "math sets," are usually scarce since few parents can afford to buy these items for all their children. These conditions are especially difficult in the primary schools, which are barely able to cope with the high numbers of enrollment on the budgets allocated to them.

The approximate enrollment in 1982 in Ebiama schools is 530— 370 in the primary school and 160 in the secondary school. The total in the three Amakiri schools is around 2,000, with 1,500 in the primary school, 400 in Okosibo Secondary School, and 150 in the girls' secondary school. Almost all the students in the primary schools of both communities are local residents; the two secondary schools have a number of students from neighboring villages.

Because of financial difficulties, the state governments have imposed levies on secondary school students. The fees vary from one term to another and usually amount to around ten naira per student per term, or thirty naira per school year. While this seems to be a relatively small amount, it represents a considerable drain for people with low incomes and who may have up to ten children in school at any one time. Parents must also provide the children with two sets of the appropriate school uniform and special shoes, all of which adds up to a large burden for many families.

All the teachers in Ebiama are Ijo, except for the headmaster of the primary school. Only one other of the twenty-six registered primary school teachers and two of the six secondary school teachers are not natives of Ebiama. By contrast, most of the teachers in the Amakiri schools are not natives of the town, nor are they Ijo. All of them come from Bendel state, however, usually from nearby Isoko and Urhobo areas. This is due to a national policy directing the states to employ teachers who were trained in that particular state. Since Bendel has a large Isoko and Urhobo population clustered around the delta, compared to the number of Ijo, it is not surprising that there are not enough Ijo teachers for all the Ijo towns. The headmaster of the primary school is an Ijo from Amakiri, but the two secondary school principals are Urhobos, as are the two vice-principals. There are about sixty teachers in the primary school and approximately thirty and ten respectively in Okosibo and the girls' secondary schools. Of this, there are about ten Amakiri natives. The teachers' level of training varies, with the younger ones possessing higher degrees or certificates than the older ones, but all of them qualified as teachers either in the primary or in the secondary schools.

The curriculum of Nigerian schools is based on a European model, with some modifications. Classes in the primary school are designed to teach the basic skills of reading, writing, and arithmetic, with some additional subjects in geography, home economics, and religion. The first two grades in the secondary school are devoted to "basic studies" and consist of general science, general social science, English literature and grammar, Bible knowledge, history, and home economics. In form 3, specialization begins and students are offered the choice of concentration in humanities, social science, or science, depending on their future career plans. This specialization determines the subjects they will eventually elect to take on the West African School Certificate examination after completing form 5. Specialization in the Amakiri and Ebiama schools is rudimentary at best, due to the lack of equipment and of teachers qualified in the various subjects, mostly science. This results in instruction in all five forms proceeding along a basic, general level.

The modifications of the basic European curriculum model represent concessions to the students' African heritage. Subjects such as West African history and geography are included, and primary school geography concentrates on the respective states in which each community is located. The new arithmetic textbooks use West African situations in their problem sets. In English literature, Nigerian writers such as Chinua Achebe and Wole Soyinka are read, along with Lamb's *Tales from Shakespeare*.

A sharp contrast between the schools in the two communities is the language of instruction. In Ebiama the primary school classes are conducted in the vernacular, and even though the upper classes are taught in English almost all the students are more comfortable speaking Ijo than English. Only one student, who had lived in Lagos, had difficulty understanding Ijo. In Amakiri the only language of instruction is English, or the local, slightly pidginized version of it. There are no classes or instruction in any of the vernaculars because of the complicated ethnic situation of the town. The Ijo majority claims the town "belongs" to them and would like to have Ijo taught in the primary school as well as in some of the secondary school classes, but this would leave the Isoko and Urhobo children, who represent about one-third of the schools' population, out of the classes, with no space for their own language instruction. Furthermore, most of the teachers are non-Ijo speakers. By the time Amakiri students finish secondary school, therefore, they are far more confident in speaking English or pidgin than Ijo, much to the chagrin of their parents. The question of language instruction in the schools is one of the major items of contention between the Amakiri Ijos and the Isoko and Urhobo in-migrants.

The Africanization of the content of some of the courses notwithstanding, the structure of the educational system and the philosophy guiding it remain European. The knowledge the children acquire is abstract and removed from the context of their life. Apart from the "three Rs," very little practical information is transmitted that would prepare those who drop out after primary school for living in a rural environment. The secondary schools are geared toward preparing students for higher education, not for any sort of occupation or practical application after graduation. How many students actually advance to postsecondary schooling is examined later.

Apart from the formal agenda, consisting of classes, requirements, and exams, schools also have an informal agenda, and influence students' behavior in and perception of less tangible areas, such as values and human relations. The schoolchildren's daily involvement in the classroom, especially the boys' involvement, disengages them from the lives of their parents. Schoolboys, although they continue in their younger years to assist with household chores, do not observe their father's occupations as relevant to their own futures—unless they are teachers, of course. The situation of the schoolgirls is slightly different and perhaps more difficult. The present generation of secondary school girls is the first one to be schooled at this level as a cohort. With a very few exceptions all their mothers are illiterate and speak no English. Since there is no question of the girls not assisting around the house, a situation results in which the girls are exposed to two very different environments involving different sets of behaviors and expectations.

The school system does not consciously lead students to question traditional authority and norms; nevertheless some practices do result in this. As we saw, within the families, the children are ranked according to age and sex, with older children and males ranking higher. The children in school are ranked on the basis of achievement. Children learn that those with ability and diligence may win promotion and prizes and surpass older ones, giving credence to the notion that rewards are based on achieved rather than ascribed criteria.

The authority of teachers is one that has also moved students to question the traditional basis of authority in the town. Their authority introduces another criterion not based on age or sex; it refers to knowledge. Most teachers are young and some of them are female, yet they know more about the subjects they teach than men older than themselves. Questioning traditional criteria for authority, however, does not result in students automatically giving deference to the new authority figures. Many teachers have a difficult time enforcing discipline in the school primarily because of their unwillingness to put enough effort into what they perceive as a frustrating occupation. The poor facilities and lack of supplies have already been mentioned. Teachers are poorly paid and sometimes do not receive their paychecks for months. Amakiri is not considered to be a desirable assignment, and Ebiama even less so, which helps to account for the high percentage of Ebiama natives on the staff. Most teachers would prefer living in an urban area. The general disaffection of many of the teachers, their lack of enthusiasm, frequent absences, and poor performance, communicates itself to the students. Students misbehave in school, cut classes, and are chronically late. Teachers respond, in their attempt to maintain order, with threats or actual physical punishment, which further erodes what little respect is left for teachers.

The school year, which is divided into three terms separated by two shorter breaks and by one long summer vacation, has altered the schoolchildren's perception of time. Whereas the rhythm of life for their parents was based on the division of year into rainy and dry seasons, which influenced what agricultural or building activities could proceed, the young people's year-round activities are unaffected by seasonal variations. For them, the major difference is between "school time" and "holiday." During holidays, and especially during the summer holiday, many of them find time on their hands, given that this is the rainy season, when planting and harvesting activities are at a standstill. It is also a slow time for house building or hauling on the river. As a result, many of the students travel around the country during these periods, visiting married sisters or brothers, and relatives as far away as Benin City, Lagos, or Port Harcourt.

To some extent, traveling to urban areas is not as much of a new experience for Amakiri youngsters as it is for those in Ebiama. For at least two generations there has been out-migration into the large urban centers, and children have been sent to live with relatives in these places, where they were schooled in return for their services in the house. What is new is the pattern of traveling in which a large number of school-age children go in and out of town, for a short period of time and for the purpose of fun and entertainment, not for work or schooling. Of the total number of adolescents questioned in Amakiri, only two were found (both of them twelve-year-old boys) who had never lived or visited elsewhere. The rest of them regularly visit Ughelli, Warri, Port Harcourt, Onitsha, and Benin and many have been as far as Lagos, Ibadan, Kano, Kaduna, and Jos. In Ebiama the situation was almost the opposite. Apart from the youth who had grown up in Lagos and several who had lived in Cameroun on fishing expeditions with their parents, 86 percent (48 females and 41 males) had resided only in Ebiama or other Ijo villages; 14 percent (8 females and 7 males) had lived outside the delta. The farthest place visited by a majority of the youngsters was Port Harcourt, sometimes only for a few days. Fifty-five percent (19 females and 18 males) had never gone beyond the clan perimeter. Like many of those who had gone to Port Harcourt for a short visit, those who had ventured to

Yenagoa, the mainland port closest to Ebiama, returned the same day.

The relationships between the towns and the school staffs are good, for the most part. From the time of their introduction, the schools were welcomed and interpreted as a progressive gesture, designed to help the community and its members. Education as an idea is highly valued and is seen as a means for social and economic betterment. Especially since the introduction of free education, fathers without exception insist that all their children take advantage of this opportunity. As a matter of fact, the idea of free education for all has rooted itself so much in the consciousness of the adults that they consider it their right. In the past few years this "right" has increasingly been questioned by the federal government, as continuing high birth rates and the post–oil boom economic crisis make it difficult to maintain the system. The state governments have started to impose levies on the secondary school children, and there is fear that the same will be necessary in the primary schools.

In Amakiri the levies are collected by the Parents and Teachers Association, which is composed of the most influential males in the community and two or three vocal women traders. Apart from collecting the levies and helping to organize graduation exercises, their role in the schools is minimal. They have no impact on the curriculum and have not even been able to help resolve the controversy surrounding the teaching of the vernaculars.

Although most parents actively encourage their children to attend school and to continue their education as long as possible, their understanding of what the school can do varies. Most of the fathers have had some schooling and wish that they had more. For them education represented a significant opportunity for guaranteed employment and often the attainment of positions of importance. Their generation came of age in the decades immediately before and after independence, when the transfer of power from the British and the growth of industries provided almost unlimited chances for advancement for educated young Nigerians. They personally witnessed the experiences of their more fortunate brothers who have managed to complete their education and are now lawyers and doctors. Consequently, they exhort their children to take advantage of the educational opportunities without considering that times have changed and that a primary or even a secondary school diploma no longer guarantees employment.

Daughters also receive encouragement to attend school since it is "free," as long as it does not stop them from performing their usual household chores. As soon as schooling interferes with these other duties, however, they are withdrawn for shorter or longer periods. Girls' primary occupation is still considered marriage and motherhood, although an ever-increasing number are managing to combine this with a profession. As far as most fathers are concerned, this is agreeable, as long as the daughters' expenses and schedules do not interfere with the schooling of their sons.

The actual burden, however, of schooling the children falls most heavily on the mothers, who provide their food and clothing. Mothers also consider education for their sons to be of first priority and are willing to sacrifice and work extra hard toward this goal. Education for the daughters, however, puzzles many of them. With the introduction of levies, their support for the daughters' education quickly evaporates, unless they have no sons.

How to Get on after School

Completing six years of primary school opens the way for further schooling or for low-level employment, such as a messenger in the civil service. To continue their education, students can enter a secondary school, a teachers training school, or a trade school. Individuals who want to teach in primary schools enter a teachers training college and graduate in five years with a teacher's certificate. The trade schools or vocational training schools offer training in catering, carpentry, shop, stenography, and typing, among other things. These courses usually take one year.

Secondary school education is intended to qualify the graduates for higher level employment or for further studies. To pursue the latter, the candidates must choose between a number of examinations which are nationally administered. Depending on the particular exam and on the score the student has received, a student may enter one of the institutions of higher education, such as the polytechnics, a college of education, a school for nursing and midwifery, or a university.

All secondary schools administer the West African School Certificate examination to their graduating form 5, or S.S. 5, students every June. The exam is given in all the subjects offered in the secondary schools, of which the candidates usually choose eight. To qualify for the certificate, they must pass in any six subjects. The General Certificate of Education (GCE) exam, ordinary level ("O-level"), is also offered once a year to any person who wishes to take it, regardless of the number of years of schooling completed. This exam, which is considered to be approximately equivalent to the West African School Certificate exam, was originally devised for individuals who have neither access nor time to attend secondary school. In fact, since it may be taken in any year, secondary school students have begun to take it instead of waiting for the West African School Certificate test in their final year of school. To receive the GCE certificate, candidates must also pass six subjects. Not passing in all six, but only in two or three, still provides an advantage and qualifies the candidate for a low-level clerical assistant's job. Candidates may take the exam as many times as they wish, until they either are satisfied with their score or give up.

A pass on the GCE Ordinary levels or on the West African School Certificate exam opens up employment as an officer in the civil service. A high-level pass qualifies a student for entry into a university, provided he or she also passes the entrance exam. This type of admission to a university is known as "entry level," meaning that students must do five years of coursework, two of which are in so-called basic studies. For entry into a polytechnic, a pass suffices. Polytechnics offer diploma courses in practical subjects, much like the trade schools, but on a higher level. Admission to the school of nursing and midwifery is similar. Those who aspire to be secondary school teachers usually enter a college of education after completing a secondary school and passing either one of the above exams with a "pass." After three years of education courses, they take the National Certificate of Education (NCE) exam. In some rare cases, an alternate route into the college of education may be from the teachers training colleges, provided the candidate passes the GCE ordinary level exam at the highest level.

The GCE advanced examination ("A-level") is more difficult than the O-level exam and usually not attempted before completing a secondary school, and then only by students who want higher education. Candidates must pass two or three subjects on this higher level to receive the A-level certificate but may take the rest of their subjects on the O-level, to complete a pass in a total of six subjects. An equivalent qualification to the GCE advanced level is provided by the Higher School Certificate (HSE), which requires two additional years of schooling after form 5 or S.S. 5 is completed, in a special secondary school or a school of basic studies. The HSE and the GCE A-levels allow for "direct entry" into a university, meaning that the candidate can skip the first two years of basic studies and immediately begin course work in his or her chosen subjects, graduating in three years.

Whether a young person's future plans include immediate employment after primary or secondary school or further education, youths in both Amakiri and Ebiama know that without a patron there is little likelihood of success. Employment opportunities are limited, regardless of qualifications, and without an influential person's help, the chances for securing a job are virtually nil. This is equally true in the civil service and in the private sector. Assistance is also needed if a youngster wants to continue his or her education. The expenses for room and board, clothes, and books are beyond the capacities of most Amakiri and Ebiama families. Since there are no scholarships for promising students, no loans or after-school employment, financing education away from home is a serious problem that is solved only with the help of other family members.

In the past, children whose parents wanted them educated beyond the classes offered in the two towns were sent to stay with relatives who were traders or worked for British companies in larger towns. Living away from home usually lasted only for a few years, but sometimes it extended into long periods, during which time the youngsters saw their parents and hometown only on rare occasions. In exchange for the room and board given them, the schoolchildren offered their manual labor in the households. Since the Amakiri and Ebiama schools were extended to offer the full range of primary and secondary classes, the practice of sending children away has been discontinued to a large extent. The schoolchildren can now stay at home and attend classes at the parents' expense. There are some exceptions. For example, if a woman living in, say Lagos, needs help in her household, she may send for her younger sister and the traditional arrangements will prevail whereby the older sister bears all the expenses of the younger one's schooling.

For higher education, support for a promising student usually came in the past from members of the extended family or descent group; it was not solely the parents' problem. In Amakiri, in particular, the larger families sought collectively to sponsor at least one son who would in turn educate his younger brothers. In this manner, Makido's leading families have managed to educate their members, to establish many of their sons in positions of prominence, and to offer various opportunities to others. To some extent this system still functions, and many graduates of the Amakiri schools can count on help from a family member. Over time, however, the traditional ties of obligation to the extended family become looser, and many successful men living in the towns are no longer willing to give unqualified and unlimited support to their Amakiri relatives. Although they are relatively well paid, living in towns is expensive and their first priority is to sponsor their own children's education. This change in attitudes has put the future plans of many of today's youngsters in Amakiri into serious jeopardy and has caused a great deal of bitterness between family members. In Ebiama, expectations for help were never high in the first place because fewer sons of the town had achieved significant success living away.

Even though the expected support extended previously for all aspiring students may not be forthcoming as a matter of course in Amakiri, many enterprising youngsters have figured out ways to secure patronage. A clever youngster will not wait until after graduation and for the family to decide what help he will be offered. He starts to establish a special relationship with a chosen individual, usually an influential uncle or a favorite older brother, early in his school career. When the chosen person visits, the youngster offers his services and tries to appear useful in various ways. He will carry the older person's bathwater, wash his clothes, shop for him, and carry his messages. Girls will similarly wait on an older sister or aunt. During vacations these students visit the older relative and gradually a mutually beneficial relationship is established. In exchange for the general usefulness and services of the youth, the older person comes to sponsor him through school or find him employment. The major difference between this system and the previous one is that the new type of sponsorship is based on individual ties and not solely on family membership.

ASPIRATIONS AND REALITY

The communities' enthusiastic response to the building of schools and their support of education has been conditioned, to a large extent, by the experience of a previous generation. As we saw earlier, Western-style education reached the Niger Delta in slow stages, for several decades providing educational opportunities to only a select few. During the first half of this century, particularly talented or tenacious youngsters, those who could find sponsors or whose families were willing to invest in the education of at least one son, managed to complete standard 6 and a very few went on to higher schools. Until the 1950s, there were no Western Ijo university students, the first one graduating from Ibadan University in 1954. Education was considered a rare commodity, leading to a better life, and to some extent in both communities, but especially in Ebiama, it continues to be so. To our knowledge, no student from Ebiama has yet graduated from a university.

Much of the promise of education was fulfilled as national independence approached, and the civil service and the economy came to be placed increasingly in the hands of Nigerians. Educated native sons were sought for important jobs. The situation was even more favorable after independence, when the country's administration was taken over in its entirety by Nigerians. Western Ijo, who were an ethnic minority in Western, and later Midwest, state, were in a particularly favorable position to place their educated sons into key government jobs since the new laws called for representation by all ethnic groups in all sectors of government. As expected, these individuals repaid their family debt by helping their younger brothers through school, many of whom also managed to secure prominent places in administration or as doctors and lawyers. The life-style of this educated elite contrasts sharply with that of their relatives, who either remained in Amakiri or migrated to towns but had to look for employment without the benefit of education.

Today's generation of schoolchildren are descendants of those who stayed home and were themselves not afforded an opportunity for advanced schooling. Their fathers' perceptions of the uses of education having been conditioned by the experiences of their own generation, it is not surprising that they think their sons' best chances for success lay in the direction of obtaining advanced schooling. The children seem to accept this position and make plans accordingly. To what extent these aspirations are fulfilled under the conditions prevailing today will be examined later, after first looking at the plans our subjects make for their future.

One consequence of the community's enthusiasm for education is that almost all children of the appropriate ages are enrolled in the primary schools. Even though many of them dropped out for some years and others proceeded at a slow pace, the vast majority of children eventually graduate from primary school. A significant percentage of primary school graduates go on to secondary school. The exact numbers are difficult to determine since many of the primary school graduates leave the community and either work or continue schooling elsewhere. Those primary school graduates who remain in the community and are not enrolled in secondary school are most frequently girls who are married or pregnant, and boys who did poorly in school and now work at odd jobs, while living in the family compound. The dropout rate from secondary school for males is low compared to that of females, many of whom drop out in the second or third years. Some of them return after one or two years; most will not.

In Amakiri, when asked about their immediate plans, all the youngsters, without exception, regardless of sex or age, said they intended to finish secondary school. As far as their occupational aspirations are concerned, the boys' answers included the following: lawyer (6), engineer (4), businessman (2), teacher (2), pilot (2), doctor (1), driver of caterpillar tractor (1), higher education with no specific occupational plans (3), and don't know (3). The girls' choices were nurse (4), teacher (4), lawyer (1), engineer (1), policewoman (1), broadcasting (1), tailoring (1), catering (1), higher education with no specific occupational plans (7), and don't know (4).

In the context of a more lengthy interview, a smaller group of somewhat older youngsters were asked similar questions. This group included 7 boys ranging from fifteen to nineteen years of age and 6 girls whose ages were fourteen to eighteen years. Every one of these youngsters expressed a desire to continue education beyond secondary school. The boys' choices included lawyer (2), businessman (1), geologist (1), engineer (1), doctor (1), and any kind of university training (1). The girls chose nursing (3), office work (1), catering (3), and a university degree (1).

As these choices show, the aspirations of most of our Amakiri adolescents are not constrained by pragmatic considerations of finances or admission requirements of higher schools. There is a difference, however, in the occupational choices of boys and girls which reflects the experience of the previous generations. Boys are much more likely to be attracted by occupations that require university training or training in an institute of higher education than are girls. Girls' plans for further education are more likely to include attendance in a polytechnic or a professional school, such as nursing or teachers training. An additional difference between boys and girls is that fewer girls have definite occupational aspirations.

When asked about the financial support they expected for these plans, every one of these thirteen youngsters named a specific individual whom they considered their sponsor. For the boys, in six cases this person was a patrilineal male relative and in one case a senior sister. The girls named four patrilineal male relatives, one male relative in the mother's patriline, and one girl named her mother.

The aspirations for schooling and occupation expressed by Ebiama youth may be said to be more limited, or more pragmatic, than those stated by their cohorts in Amakiri. Of 17 female respondents, 15 said they would continue in school as long as they were sponsored and as long as schooling was needed to obtain employment. Two said they did not know how much more schooling they desired. The employment objectives were as follows: 7 want to be teachers, 2 want to be nurses, 2 want to be employed in some fashion (including 1 whose mother has not told her yet what she should be), 1 gave marriage as her future occupation goal, and 5 said they had no idea as to what they wanted to do. The male respondents were more specific in their educational objectives. Of 24 male respondents, all except one said they wanted to complete secondary school and continue on to college or the university. The exception said he did *not* want to go to secondary school. Nevertheless, like the females, their occupational goals were limited or not yet formed. Only 4 named a professional title (lawyer, doctor, engineer); 1 said "big man," indicating he wanted to be a politician; 7 want to be teachers, 3 radio mechanics; 1 soldier; 1 civil servant; and 7 did not know yet.

When the individuals in Amakiri were asked where they would like to live when older, an overwhelming majority stated that they would like to live in a bigger town, away from Amakiri. The reasons given included more job opportunities, more entertainment, electricity, or because a favorite brother or sister lived there. The only subjects who expressed a desire to remain in their home community were those who wanted to be teachers. Given the occupational aspirations of these youngsters and the lack of opportunities in Amakiri, the answers again reflect the experience of the previous generations where becoming a successful professional meant moving to a bigger town, as a matter of course. By the same reasoning we find that the Ebiama youth see Ebiama as their future home. Only one male, who had grown up in Lagos, wanted to reside in a city. Others wanted to move away from Ebiama, but unlike Amakiri they were not attracted away as much as they were expressing unhappiness at living in the village.

An additional question regarding future plans revealed another difference in the views of our boys and girls, and between the two communities. The subjects were asked about their marital plans—whether they wanted to be married in polygamous or monogamous unions—and the number of children they wished to have. In Amakiri the majority (eighteen) of the girls said they would prefer to be married polygynously, whereas the majority (sixteen) of the boys stated they only wanted one wife. Many of the girls who wanted co-wives felt that to be successful as a woman one had to be married to a "big man" who had a large household with many children. Others, however, viewed co-wives as helpmates who share cooking and other household chores, thereby making it possible for one another to continue schooling or trading. These views are shared by those boys who wanted to marry polygynously and who considered a polygynous household a sign of success. The majority of the boys, however, had no desire to head such a household, and equated success and happiness with one wife who is educated. These boys thought that many wives are troublesome, and while they may make each other's lives easier, they are difficult for a man to control. Somewhat along the same lines, more girls expressed a desire to have more children, up to ten or "as many as God gives," than boys, the majority of whom wanted three to six children. These gender differences seem to reflect the successful role models that for girls are most often women who are married to big men in polygynous unions.

In Ebiama the female respondents were shy in replying to questions about marriage and children. Seven said they wanted two, three, or many co-wives; ten gave no preference, but none said they wanted to be their husband's only wife. Fifty percent of the males (twelve) said they wanted two wives, six only wanted to marry one wife, and six did not know how many. Those giving a preference, whether one or two, said they did not want more because of the arguments caused by having two or three wives and because of the expense.

Most of the career choices voiced by the Amakiri youngsters require completion of secondary school and passing the West African School Certificate exam or the General Certificate of Education (GCE), Ordinary Level. We obtained the grades from Okosibo Secondary School for the years when records were kept to examine how previous classes had fared. Records were not available in Ebiama since classes were still being added to the secondary school. The grades for the West African School Certificate exam were available between 1977 and 1980 only, because in 1981 the entire class took the GCE Ordinary Level, and the 1982 grades were not yet recorded at the time of the study. The passing score, which is the average of scores on six subjects, for the West African Certificate of Education exam is 45. In 1977 three out of five passed; in 1978, one out of three; in 1979, two out of six; in 1980, all five failed. The highest recorded passing score during this period was 53.

To receive the GCE Ordinary Level, a student must pass, as mentioned earlier, at least six subjects. Thirteen students took the exam in 1981. None received a certificate, but three of them did pass five of the subjects. Those with the highest passes still did not qualify for schools other than nursing or teachers training or for low-level civil service jobs.

To examine what occupations are opened up for our youngsters with the education obtained in the Amakiri schools and to see the extent to which the stated aspirations of our respondents were realistic, we tried to collect information on their older brothers' and sisters' careers. Table 8.1 shows the employment status and/or educational choices of an unsystematic sample of school leavers from the Makido quarters between 1975 and 1981.

Those students from Makido who completed form 5 in 1982 stayed around the community for most of the research period, and their subsequent activities were monitored. There were fourteen Makido youngsters who completed secondary school in that year, of whom approximately half were part of the study sample. There were three girls and eleven boys among the graduates. Of the fourteen, five boys remained in Amakiri, waiting for the result of their exams, eventually deciding to retake them. Two boys entered the School of Basic Studies in Port Harcourt, hoping to take the Higher School Certificate exam upon its completion. One boy took a job as clerk with a company in Warri, and another obtained temporary work in Port Harcourt. Two other boys went to stay with relatives in Lagos, hoping to find employment. Of the three girls, two gave birth soon after graduation and one moved to Warri where she is staying with relatives.

Comparing the occupational aspirations of our sample of thirty-two boys and thirty-one girls with the careers of their brothers and

TABLE 8.1

Occupations of Amakiri Students Graduating or Leaving School between 1975 and 1981

	MALE	FEMALE
Primary school graduates/secondary school dropouts		
Unemployed/odd jobs	6	—
Marriage &/or pregnant unemployed	—	15
Laborer	1	—
Hospital orderly	—	1
Vocational training school	3	—
Transport (boat, bus)	2	—
Military	1	—
Secondary school graduates		
Unemployed/odd jobs	5	3
Marriage/no job	—	2
Transport	1	—
Clerk	5	2
Military	1	—
Teachers training school	6	4
College of education	4	1
Midwifery school	—	1
Nursing school	—	2
Polytechnic	4	—
University	4	1

sisters, twenty-one males chose occupations that would require a university degree; the rest of them, with one exception, selected fields that necessitate higher education in an institution other than a university. Approximately half of their older brothers were university graduates. Of the thirty-one females, twenty-one wanted to attend institutions of higher education, three of which were university. About half of their older sisters realized this level of education. While the girls' aspirations are somewhat lower than those of the boys, the majority of them still want higher education. When these career choices are compared with the postgraduation experiences of the class of 1982, the picture seems even bleaker since no member of that class has managed to find satisfactory employment or had test scores high enough to enter a higher educational institution. The aspirations of both male and female subjects in the sample are high regardless of the example of their older siblings (Hollos 1987).

While a considerable number of Amakiri secondary school

graduates continue schooling in an institute of higher education (the majority of them in Teacher Training College), an equally high number are unemployed. Their unemployment rate is comparable to that of the primary school graduates. Those who managed to secure employment after graduating from secondary school work as low-level clerks. The situation is even more pessimistic in Ebiama because there is no older cohort of secondary school graduates to turn to for help.

Part of the reason for the relatively low success rate in obtaining jobs and in entering schools of higher education undoubtedly lies with the students whose examination scores are below the national average. The major cause, however, is the economic and political situation in the country and the consequent shrinking opportunities for middle-level white collar jobs. Today's youth compare themselves to that of their fathers' generation which came of age at a time of almost unlimited opportunities, albeit not always for their own fathers, who seem to believe that the conditions of the past are still the same and therefore are unable to give realistic guidance to the younger generation. Without perceptive parental advice, and with the school system still operating in full gear, the majority of youth simply continue on a path that not so long ago was considered to be a guaranteed way to a successful life, but now appears to lead to unemployment and frustration.

■ Conclusion

Adolescence, as a distinct period of life, has received ample attention from Western psychiatrists, psychologists, and sociologists (for example, Freud 1949; Hall 1904; Erikson 1963, 1968; Piaget 1965; Inhelder and Piaget 1958; Kohlberg 1969, 1976). Even though these authorities, who represent varied theoretical perspectives, are not in consensus on the characteristics of this period, they seem to agree on two major points: one, that adolescence is a universally recognizable distinct stage in the life cycle, and two, that its major defining characteristics are the emotional, cognitive, and social readjustments that are brought about by the physiological changes at puberty. In the words of Peter Blos, this "increase in psychological differentiation during adolescence is necessarily attended by an increase in psychic lability. This condition is reflected by adolescent emotional disturbances of varying seriousness and crippling effects, transient or permanent" (1962, 9).

Our work with the youth of two Ijo communities in Nigeria was not designed necessarily to challenge this view, but to offer an ethnographic description of young people coming into adulthood in a non-Western society and thereby to add to the information available on this life stage. By looking at their experience, we hope we can examine the way social conditions influence the development of this stage as a recognized entity and thereby question our assumptions about the inevitability of some of its characteristics.

If we were to take a microscopic view of this age period by

149

examining the differences between Ebiama and Amakiri alone, we would conclude that variations in the context of society and culture have little effect on the behavioral manifestations of adolescence. To be sure, there are differences: the Amakiri youth are more sophisticated than their Ebiama counterparts in their knowledge and experience of the urban centers and the kinds of occupations to which they aspire. The strategy they use also differs. To attain their goals they center their attention on patrilineal kinsmen, many of whom have already achieved prominent roles. The kinsmen whom Ebiama adolescents look to for assistance are found in both the mother's and father's descent groups, and, because of the isolation of Ebiama and its smaller population, there is a smaller pool of people of prominence in the older generation on which to draw. Other differences, such as those found in the questionnaires directed toward gender preference, are minor compared to the overwhelming emphasis and value placed on the male role compared to the female role. The similarities between the youth in both communities are such that in most instances we were able to use one description to encompass the two. Even where we might expect to find a difference because of a sharply contrasting cultural feature, such as the presence of clitoridectomy in Amakiri and its absence in Ebiama, there is no discernible variation in the value placed on premarital sex or pregnancy (Hollos and Leis 1986). Of more consequence is the similarity in the environment of growing up in extended families, with their emphasis on acceptance and security, while at the same time individuals are expected to assume responsibilities and perform tasks that make them independent of surrogates at an early age.

CHANGES

Traditional Ijo society recognized a number of named stages in the life cycle, none of which corresponded to Western ideas of adolescence. The stages were somewhat different for boys and for girls, indicating the different experiences and expectations of the sexes.

Young girls were called *eruoba* (girl) from age six to about age twelve. As a girl approached puberty she was expected to move to her future husband's compound, marry, and advance to the next stage, the *ereso*, or "young 'nubile' woman." Thus, for girls there was no period of transition between being a child and a married woman. There were no rituals marking this change in status, nor the onset of the first menses. Gifts were exchanged and money was paid at the time of marriage, but they were not designed to celebrate the woman's coming of age. Rather, they indicated that her sexual and, depending on the form of marriage in Ebiama, her reproductive capacities were being transferred to her husband and his descent group. The only ritual designed to mark a woman's change of status occurred in Amakiri, where her clitoridectomy and the segbein, her "coming out" dance, were associated with her fertility and the achievement of motherhood, which, in a sense, was synonymous with adult womanhood.

Boys married later than girls since the traditional occupations they needed to learn required the strength that comes with physical maturation, and therefore to establish even a semi-independent household required some years. Boy, as did girls, entered a new life stage at age six, that of *kala awou* (young boys), but remained in it longer than girls, usually until they were considered big or strong enough to partake in communal work projects and to become accepted among the *kala pesi* (young persons). In Ebiama the ceremony performed when a boy successfully cut down his first bunch of palm fruit was a good indication that he had arrived at this stage. The kala pesi were the muscle of the community and performed all the hard work under the direction of the elders. Boys remained in this group until their midtwenties, when they usually married and assumed the responsibilities of adult males. Although the entrance and exit from the kala pesi stage were not marked by rituals as in many other African societies, it was a time for learning future roles and acquiring new responsibilities. The conceptualization of this period differed from our notions of adolescence in that instead of being a liminal period, it was looked on as one of hard work and serious preparation for adult life. It may be said to resemble our period of adolescence, at least for males, in that both were extended well beyond the teenage years.

The past twenty-five years in Nigeria witnessed an increasingly accelerating process of social and economic change as the country moved from a colonial agrarian society to an independent, industrializing nation. The expansion of communication networks, the introduction and expansion of Western-style schooling, and the shift from primary occupations to wage labor impacted on the traditional life-styles and cultural values at an unprecedented rate. Ijo youths were effected primarily through the educational system, introduced into African societies as a major instrument of development and change. In Ijo society, as well as in the rest of Nigeria, the rapid growth of schooling resulted in the creation of a new set of expectations among the youth coming of age under the new system. It also resulted in a restructuring of the traditional life cycle by providing a prolonged period of schooling to girls and a reinterpretation of learning and preparation for boys.

The age labels in contemporary usage refer to schooling as a criterion for defining the boundaries of an age period. Girls who in earlier times would have been classified as ereso and would have been married, today still live in their parental compounds and attend secondary school. There is no appropriate label available for them in the traditional terminological system, and they are therefore known as "big schoolgirls." The term *ereso* is now reserved for girls who have finished schooling, by which time they are usually seventeen or eighteen years old. The introduction of the new label signifies the development of a new substage between childhood and adulthood and the prolongation of the period before marriage. For boys, being called kala pesi now implies secondary schooling, and the term is used as a synonym for "big schoolboy." Being a schoolboy, however, is a far less serious enterprise than being a young apprentice male was in former times, and so the meaning of this life stage has changed to one closely approximating our own notion of "adolescence." For both sexes, the introduction of Western-style schooling has resulted in a prolonged period of what may be called adolescence, with changed behavioral requirements and different expectations for the future from their parents. In this society, they are the first generation to experience this period of transition as a cohort, rather than as a few individuals, and also the first to be prepared for identifying themselves selves first as Nigerians, rather than as Ijos. The lesson is learned, however, as a continuation of past experience.

CONTINUITIES

If the introduction of Western-style schooling resulted in the creation of a period of adolescence in the Ijo life cycle, in what sense do the behaviors and experiences of Ijo adolescents resemble those of their Western counterparts? The major question is whether the emotional, cognitive, and social readjustments which are thought to be necessary undertakings in this period necessarily bring about similar anxieties, conflicts, and testing of limits in Ijo adolescents as they do in Western youngsters?

In looking at this stage among the Ijo, one important fact emerges: while adolescence as a life stage is a new invention in this society, it has occurred in the context of Ijo culture, utilizing traditional behavior patterns. In experiencing this transition, youngsters refer to and utilize existing cultural norms and expectations to interpret and fashion newly emerging behaviors.

At birth, an Ijo infant enters a web of kinship that defines his or her rights and obligations, the outer limits of the world of significant others, and the rules by which this world operates. These relationships and rules follow the individual throughout life, and while their weight and significance may shift, he or she is forever embedded in a close network. The extended family acts as a buffer between the individual and the harsher realities of the village and the nation, protecting and at the same time limiting the individual's actions. The kinship system in today's changing world still operates with the same mechanisms as it did before, and primary loyalties are given to members within the family. Individuals know that as long as their behavior is within the expected bounds, someone will feed, clothe, and school them, and they expect to be called on to do the same for others. There is security in the knowledge that these relationships will never be broken and also in knowing clearly what is expected of them.

Based on the major similarities we found between the two communities, we interpret this security as having its roots in the context of extended polygynous families. The conflicts between co-wives on behalf of protecting the benefits that might accrue to their offspring from their shared husband only seem to reaffirm the interdependency of kinsmen as they face both nonkinsmen and the problems of achieving positions of importance as adults in their own community or elsewhere.

With occupational change and Western-style schooling today, youngsters, both male and female, no longer learn their adult economic roles through interaction with their parents and other adults. Generational differences are also becoming sharper as young adults talk explicitly about "modernization" and the difficulties they have in making changes in the face of conservative elders. Respect for age and elders has been, and continues to be, an important tenet of Ijo society, just as individual achievement continues to be recognized and appreciated, but in new forms. There is continuity in the tone of relations between elders and juniors that inhibits attempts to challenge the elders' authority. This is not to say that Ijo youngsters do not distinguish between traditional village elders and those who are more successful in modern Nigerian society and to whom they can turn for help and support. Still, both types of elders continue to receive respect and deference. In such a society, adolescents grow up knowing who they are and what others expect of them; there is no need to test limits and to show off, since their obligations and expectations are marked out for them. A clever, good student who wishes to advance can do so, but his or her advancement will be achieved by finding a sponsor among the members of the kin group and by demonstrating loyalty and respect for the sponsor.

In our conceptualization of adulthood in the West, we tend to assume that to become an adult the individual must be autonomous and independent. The terms are used almost synonymously, even though they convey quite different meanings. Autonomy is defined as being dissociated from a primary group in psychological, social and economic terms. Independence, on the other hand, refers to the ability to initiate action on one's own, to make choices and take responsibility for decisions. Western adolescents, to be autonomous, must stress their independence. They are expected to sever their linkages to their kin group, go off to college in a distant place, or take an apartment when they start work.

In our understanding of the Ijo situation, this connection between the two concepts is not present. While independence is important, autonomy is not an issue. Ijo adults and adolescents are embedded in a kinship network which they do not see as interfering with the achievement of adulthood. On the contrary, a person's self-identity is bound up with a feeling of continuity with the past, with the kin group and its ancestors, which positions each person in society. Youngsters express this feeling by stating their desire to have large families of their own since they consider it important "to have people behind them." This reference has a double meaning. It expresses the power of numbers, since a large group can fight or compete more successfully than a small group. It also expresses the power of memory. The deceased are remembered as long as there are living descendents to honor them. To establish identity, what is important is not separation from kin groups but knowing that one is part of them.

Independence is a different issue altogether and does not contradict the above. For the Ijo to achieve independence, there is no need to separate and disembed themselves from kin. Quite to the contrary, we see independence as made possible for them by their being part of a larger entity that stands behind them and supports them. Psychological studies support this contention that young children exhibit exploratory and coping behaviors more readily when they are securely attached to the mother (Bowlby 1969). Ijo children are encouraged to be self-reliant, to take initiatives, and to be responsible from an early age. Young children perform tasks, travel, change residence and friends with ease. These behaviors continue into adolescence and do not represent the introduction of a new requirement in preparation for adulthood. Independence and the ability to manage one's own affairs, to utilize one's skills in achieving goals, to acquire sponsors, and to try to find a better placement in life are continuously stressed and encouraged. These actions and decisions, however, are being made from the safety and security of a group that stands behind the individual, regardless of success or failure in worldly activities.

The emphasis on independence rather than autonomy can be found in every adolescent relationship. Peer groups, for example, acquire an overwhelming significance for Western adolescents who seek autonomy from parents and search for their own identity. In Erikson's words, they "temporarily 'overidentify,' to the point of apparent complete loss of identity, with the heroes of cliques and crowds" (1963, 262). Ijo adolescents do not look to peers for cues to forming one's identity since those cues are safely lodged in their larger kin group. As a consequence, peer relations are tenuous, peer-group membership is forever changing, and there are no stable cliques. Loyalties to friends are not long term and are based on current needs and the exchange of needed items. One's friends do not determine one's self-perception and behaviors in important ways.

The same may be said for love relationships. "Falling in love," according to Erikson, is a further attempt in the West for adolescents "to arrive at a definition of one's identity by projecting one's diffused ego image on another and by seeing it thus reflected and gradually clarified" (1963, 262). Ijo adolescents maintain a pragmatic view on the matter. Love and sex are fun but are not matters of life and death, and the relationships that youngsters establish are not expected to last and are not taken seriously either by them or by the older generation. What is serious, however, is ultimate mate selection, which rests primarily on considerations that have to do with the fertility and housekeeping abilities of the woman and the appropriateness of family background and finances. The value placed on polygynous marriages may also be seen as an indication that even more permanent attachments carry a more diffuse emotional load then Westerners invest in marital relations and from which they derive much of their long-term identity.

Finally, occupational identity and careers form an important component in the identity formation of Western youth. "In most instances, it is the inability to settle on an occupational identity which disturbs young people," according to Erikson (1963, 262). For Ijo youth, occupations are considered important, and all youngsters are encouraged to take advantage of the educational opportunities offered. As we saw, however, it is unclear at this point whether schooling will lead to desired careers or any kind of commensurate employment. As a rule, young people go without jobs for years, stay at home, pick up odd jobs, and eventually move to a city where, with the help of influential relatives, they work in a number of positions that only rarely achieve permanence. These difficulties are reflected in the attitude of the adolescents toward schooling. As a rule, education is not taken seriously, and the students' lack of preparation results in poor performances on the final exams. Since their identity does not hinge on occupational identity, Ijo youth appear to take these vicissitudes in stride.

The adolescent stage in Ijo society is a new invention. We see it, however, as being far less difficult and conflict ridden than in the West since its main task, the achievement of identity, is not based on the need to establish complete autonomy and to sever ties with one's kin group. These important ties continue and give a feeling of continuous situatedness throughout life. At the same time, independence of individual action is encouraged, but it does not represent a new expectation in adolescence. Independence has been a traditional Ijo value, and its inculcation is part of becoming an Ijo adult.

This relative lack of major conflicts, anxiety, and stress in Ijo adolescent life is demonstrated by a similar lack of suicide and delinquency among the youth. While there is talk of some youngsters smoking "indian hemp" (marijuana), it is difficult to elicit any names of actual users in Amakiri. The sole Amakiri youth who is widely known as a "smoker" is clearly mentally disturbed and exhibits a variety of aberrant behaviors, such as attacking his father with a broken beer bottle. His behavior, whether or not his problems are due to it, is held up as a deterrent for others who may contemplate using narcotics. A similar example is found in Ebiama, where the cause of a youth's mental illness is attributed to an overabundant use of marijuana. His case, however, has not prevented others from smoking it. Adolescent suicide is completely unknown. Delinquency is largely limited to petty theft, which is severely sanctioned and punished in Ijo society. Fights and brawls among adolescent boys are frequent but they are evidence of "normal" behavior, not of the breaking down of the social order.

THE FUTURE

In the foregoing we have emphasized the differences between Western and Ijo adolescence. In one sense, however, Ijo adolescence resembles this life stage in Western societies: in both places individuals are being trained for an uncertain future. The cultural model of "modernity" is borrowed from the West, but it is becoming increasingly clear that African societies have to make their own adjustments and find their own solutions, and that the Western model may not serve as the best example to follow in the long run. How to train the future generations for these developments is unclear, just as it is unclear in the United States and Europe, where the limitations on ever-expanding production and opportunities, and the possibility of a progressive lowering of the standard of living are becoming more evident.

In this era of change, the Ijo may have an advantage. Their experience demonstrates the potential importance of family and kin ties as a cushion against the impact of rapidly changing economic and political conditions, and as a way of being secure with one's identity by being an inalienable link of a larger group.

■ References

Abernethy, D. B. 1965. "Education and Politics in a Developing Society: The Southern Nigerian Experience." Ph.D. dissertation, Harvard University.

Alagoa, E. J. 1972. *A History of the Niger Delta: An Historical Interpretation of Ijo Oral Tradition.* Ibadan: Ibadan University Press.

Blos, Peter. 1962. *On Adolescence.* New York: Free Press.

Bowlby, John. 1969. *Attachment.* New York: Basic Books.

Bradbury, R. E. 1957. *The Benin Kingdom and the Edo-Speaking Peoples of South-Western Nigeria.* London: International African Institute.

Dike, Kenneth Onwuka. 1956. *Trade and Politics in the Niger Delta, 1830–1885: An Introduction to the Economic and Political History of Nigeria.* Oxford: Clarendon Press.

Erikson, Erik. 1963. *Childhood and Society.* Rev. ed. New York: Norton.

———. 1968. *Identity, Youth, and Crisis.* New York: Norton.

Freud, S. 1949. *An Outline of Psychoanalysis.* New York: Norton.

Guyer, Jane I. 1981. "Household and Community in African Studies." *African Studies Review* 24:87–137.

Hall, G. Stanley. 1904. *Adolescence.* New York: Appleton.

Hollos, Marida. 1987. "Education in Nigeria: Early Premises and Present Realities for Ijo Youth." Paper presented at the Annual meeting of the Northeastern Anthropological Association, Albany, N.Y., March 1987.

Hollos, Marida, and Philip E. Leis. 1986. "Descent and Permissive Adolescent Sexuality in Two Ijo Communities." *Ethos* 14, 4:395–408.

Hollos, Marida, Philip E. Leis, and Elliot Turiel. 1986. "Social Reasoning in Nigerian Children and Adolescents." *Journal of Cross-Cultural Psychology* 17, 3:352–374.

Hollos, Marida, and Francis Richards. 1988. "The Development of Formal

Operations in Nigerian Adolescents." *Journal of Cross-Cultural Psychology* (in press).

Horton, Robin. 1962. "The Kalabari World-view: An Outline and Interpretation." *Africa* 32, 3:197–219.

————. 1969. "From Fishing Village to City-State: A Social History of New Calabar." In M. Douglas and P. M. Kaberry, eds., *Man in Africa*, pp. 37–58. London: Tavistock.

Inhelder, B., and Jean Piaget. 1958. *The Growth of Logical Thinking from Childhood to Adolescence*. New York: Basic Books.

Jones, G. I. 1963. *The Trading States of the Oil Rivers*. London: Oxford University Press.

Kohlberg, L. 1969. "Stage and Sequence: The Cognitive Developmental Approach to Socialization." In D. A. Goslin, ed., *Socialization Theory*. Chicago: Rand McNally.

————. 1976. "Moral Stages and Moralization: The Cognitive Developmental Approach." In T. Lickons, ed., *Moral Development and Behavior*. New York: Holt, Rinehart & Winston.

Leis, Nancy B. 1964. "Economic Independence and Ijaw Women: A Comparative Study of Two Communities in the Niger Delta." Ph.D. dissertation, Northwestern University.

————. 1974. "Women in Groups: Ijaw Women's Associations." In M. Z. Rosaldo and L. Lamphere, eds., *Woman, Culture, and Society*, pp. 223–242. Stanford: Stanford University Press.

————. 1982. "The Not-So-Supernatural Power of Ijaw Children." In Simon Ottenberg, ed., *African Religious Groups and Beliefs*, pp. 151–169. Meerut, India: Archana Publications for the Folklore Institute.

Leis, Philip E. 1964a. "'Collective Sentiments' as Represented in Ijaw Divination." *Journal of the Folklore Institute* 1:167–179.

————. 1964b. "Palm Oil, Illicit Gin, and the Moral Order of the Ijaw." *American Anthropologist* 66:828–838.

————. 1972. "Enculturation and Socialization in an Ijaw Village." New York: Holt, Rinehart and Winston.

————. 1982. "History and Evolution in the Niger Delta." Faculty of Humanities, University of Port Harcourt, November 11, 1982. Manuscript.

Netting, Robert McC., Richard R. Wilk, and Eric J. Arnould, eds. 1984. *Households*. Berkeley: University of California Press.

O'Connell, J. 1965. "Education, Economics, and Politics." In L. Gray Cowan, James O'Connell, and David S. Scanlon, eds., *Education and Nation-Building in Africa*, pp. 187–191. New York: Praeger.

Piaget, J. 1965. *The Moral Judgement of the Child*. New York: Free Press.

Tallman, Irving, Ramona Marotz-Baden, and Pablo Pindas. 1983. *Adolescent Socialization in Cross-Cultural Perspective*. New York: Academic Press.

Turner, James. 1971. "Universal Education and Nation-building in Africa." *Journal of Black Studies* 2, 1:3–27.

Whiting, John W. M., V. K. Burbank, and M. S. Ratner. 1986. "The Duration of Maidenhood across Cultures." In J. B. Lancaster and B. A. Hamburg, eds., *School Age Pregnancy and Parenthood*, pp. 273–302. Hawthorne, New York: Aldine de Gruyter.

Whiting, John W. M., I. L. Child, and W. M. Lambert. 1966. *Field Guide for a Study of Socialization*. Six Cultures Series, vol. 1. New York: John Wiley.

Williamson, Kay. 1965. *A Grammar of the Kolokuma Dialect of Ijo*. London: Cambridge University Press.

▪ Index

major conflicts of, 156; and male attitudes toward polygyny, 145; marital plans of, 145; as mothers' helpmates, 58; and pregnancy, 124; relationship.to head of household of, 41, 51; residential choices of, 144; sexual interest of, 118; travel of, 136. *See also* adolescence